CO. ...I I I ED
TO CONFLICT

THE DESTRUCTION
OF THE CHURCH IN RWANDA

—

Laurent Mbanda
assisted by Steve Wamberg

First published in Great Britain 1997
Society for Promoting Christian Knowledge
Holy Trinity Church
Marylebone Road
London NW1 4DU

British Library Cataloguing-in-Publication Data

A catalogue record of this book is available
from the British Library

ISBN 0-281-05016-3

Typeset by Wilmaset Ltd, Wirral
Printed in Great Britain by
The Cromwell Press, Melksham, Wiltshire

To my wife Chantal, daughter Erica and sons Eric and Eddie, whose love and understanding have contributed much more than they know to the writing of this book. They have been incredibly patient in allowing me to spend most of my evening family time on the writing.

Contents

Preface

Let no more gods or exploiters be served Let us learn rather to love one another.

Francisco Ferr, Spanish free thinker

Speak boldly, and speak truly, and shame the devil.

John Fletcher

GENOCIDE PUT RWANDA on the map for most of the world.

That has been a peculiar irony for me as a native Rwandan. I have been audience to a number of people interpreting the Rwanda situation since the slaughter of April 1994, although before then, as a student and resident of the United States, I came in contact with people in academic institutions and elsewhere who had never heard of the country. When I spoke at mission conferences, I'd refer to Rwanda as 'part of what was the Belgian Congo' just so I could see a few heads nod as though they knew what I was talking about. But even that was no guarantee anyone in a given audience could get up and locate Rwanda on a globe – or an African map, for that matter.

That lack of information concerning Rwanda showed clearly in many 'expert' analyses that filled the newspapers, magazines and talk shows that followed the April 1994 genocide. Too often, the situation was dismissed as 'tribal conflict' and left me with a feeling that my countrymen were being counted as somehow subhuman in the Western world.

The tragedy of the matter is that 'tribal conflict' was virtually unknown to Rwanda before colonialism. Now, this book discloses one of the best-kept secrets of the Rwandan church to the outside world. By tracing the church–state relationship from the time Christian missionaries entered Rwanda, the book reveals the patterns of manipulations within the Church that actually nurtured hatred between the two major groups. *Committed to Conflict* traces and exposes some of the 'business as usual' principles, unwritten rules, practices, associations and decisions that went unchallenged for generations and that finally misled much of the Church

into facilitating rather than standing against genocide. That the idea of
'divide and rule' gave birth to such evil in the very country where the East
African Revival began is one of the most painful paradoxes of modern
Christianity. The 1994 genocide in the beautiful 'Land of a Thousand
Hills' saw the historical pattern prevail that has been constant since 1959:
in a country where 86 per cent of the population is supposed to be Christian, the established Church and its leadership were silent – or worse, participants – in the foment of genocide.

It is my hope and prayer that the content of this book will cause many to
think of their own context, and look at certain issues in this book with implications for the Church beyond Rwandan borders. Perhaps this may also
cause and challenge Christians, and non-Christians, to think and ask ourselves where and how we draw lines in today's pluralistic society.

Acknowledgements

I would like to acknowledge gratefully Paul Gordon Chandler, whom I have long admired, for inviting and encouraging me to write this book; Naomi Starkey, my commissioning editor, who made the initiative to contact me; and Steve Wamberg for the tremendous technical assistance, patience, persistence and perspective as a writer.

There are others for whom I owe a word of appreciation:

for Bob and Jody Lewis, who committed to hold me accountable for the writing and whose words of encouragement kept me moving

for Jean and Vivian Gakwandi's willingness to interact and discuss issues

for Aimable Gahima's comments on the manuscript

for those who read portions of the manuscript and provided useful comments

for the friendship, prayers, advice and encouragement of John T. Bass

for Todd and Dana Retting's prayers and friendship

for Alemu Beeftu's advice and encouragement

for Ted and Margaret Ward, whose influence and support I enjoyed during my graduate studies

for all my colleagues at Compassion International.

The Christian message is not being heard. After a century of evangelism we have to begin again because the best catechists, those who filled our churches on Sundays, were the first to go out with machetes in their hand.

Bishop Nsengiyumva

Part One

—

Mission and Manipulation

ONE

Double Mission:
The Colonial Masters and
Early Missionaries

NOT SO LONG ago, Rwanda was a small, mountainous country that was perhaps best known as the home of mountain gorillas. Rwanda was the most densely populated country in Africa with 7.5 million people, 285 inhabitants per square kilometre, before the 1994 genocide. In the late 1980s I remember former president Habyarimana and his politicians using the population density as an excuse for their refusal to allow the 1959 refugees to return to Rwanda.

I was one among those not allowed to return to my country of birth. I found myself resenting his political speeches, and at times angry. Being a Christian, my resentment was often brought to the Lord for forgiveness, and my statelessness for comfort. This did not mean, however, that I did not hunger to at least visit and see the homeland I was forced to leave at the age of four. Population density was no issue to me. I was stateless. That was hard and hopeless enough. I wanted to belong, to be allowed in and out of the country of my birth whether or not I lived there.

Rwanda is home to a people called the Banyarwanda, who embrace three groups – Hutu, Tutsi and Twa – of the same nation. Let me say it again: *three groups of the same nation.* Although these groups have been referred to as 'ethnic' or 'tribal' groups, they share a common language, and Rwandan elders believe that these three groups are one people with a common ancestry. As a child growing up, I heard stories from elders that the first inhabitant of Rwanda had three children. He named them Gahutu, Gatutsi and Gatwa. (*'Ga'* means 'small' in Kinyarwanda.) The average Rwandan knew of the groups that came from each of the children, and certainly identified with one of them. But the emphasis was on what they shared instead of what might divide them. The unique proof of that is the Banyarwanda living in the same village houses next to one another for centuries, sharing a common language and culture.

However, this belief does not settle well with anthropologists (and, you'll discover, early missionaries), who have laboured intensively to uncover distinct origins for each of the three groups. Tribal societies are commonly identified by divisions in language, culture and geographical boundaries – divisions that simply are not to be found in precolonial Rwandan history, even though certain areas were more populated by one of the three groups. The average Rwandan who managed to grow his food, or look after his cows, thought of the groups more in terms of castes (for want of a better word) determined by occupation. In precolonial Rwanda, the royal family, nobles, army commanders, most chiefs, and people who kept cattle, were Abatutsi (Tutsi). The Abahutu (Hutu) were generally considered to be a lower class than the Abatutsi. The Abatwa (Twa) were a distinct minority characterized by hunting and pottery-making, and considered to be somewhat on the fringe of everyday affairs.

Most people are surprised to hear that a Hutu could become a Tutsi, and vice versa. A Hutu who gained status through wealth or by becoming a chief could become a Tutsi through a ritual of *Kwihutura* – literally, a cleansing of one's Hutuness. In like manner, if a Tutsi lost his cattle, or turned to farming for a living and married into a Hutu family, that person could become Hutu. So economics are a larger consideration than ethnicity in determining whether a Rwandan is Hutu or Tutsi. Bishop Classe, one of the Catholic priests who shaped the ideology of colonial rule in Rwanda, wrote, ' "Tutsi" often refers not to origin but to social condition, or wealth, especially as regards cattle: whoever is chief, or is rich will often be referred to as Tutsi.' Intermarriage is not a recent phenomenon, either. It is a long-standing practice that further served to blur group distinctions.

That said, it cannot be denied that, among the Banyarwanda, the Tutsi formed the upper class which exercised control over the Hutu. It is not a surprising pattern among societies that the people with wealth tend to control the working class. The Tutsis' influence came from their wealth as was defined by the number of cattle they owned. Indeed, most historians have described the Tutsi dominance as a system of feudalism based on cattle. Tutsi leadership and control over the affairs of the country can be traced back to the seventeenth century. Interdependence was evident through trade of labour or crops from the Hutus to the Tutsis in exchange for milk and cattle. Still, it was easy for this system to be abused, and it developed into a form of patronage that was abused by some in power, to the extent that it required forms of protection for the less fortunate. Favour with those in power, especially in relation to the king, became a commodity. Frequently the price of protection for the Hutus was an inordinate amount of labour or crops. Even the poor among the Tutsis were oppressed by the system.

Even with this imperfect caste system in place, the Rwandan people lived together in peace until the mid-twentieth century. Precolonial Rwandan history is absent of any mention of war between the Banyarwanda groups, although there are recorded many battles between Rwanda and bordering kingdoms.

As a kingdom, Rwanda had established her status and earned the respect of her neighbours. The nation remained out of contact with the so-called 'armies of colonial occupation' until 1879, when the famous British explorer Henry Morton Stanley entered Rwanda via Gisaka. Still, real penetration of Rwanda did not take place until 1894, when Germany's Count Gustaav-Adolf Von Goetzen entered Rwanda from Tanzania and met king Rwabugiri. By 1899 the Germans took Rwanda as their colony and held it until the end of World War I, when Belgium laid claim to it. (Rwandans who remember those days recall that the Germans did not have as many people in Rwanda as Belgium had along the borders of Zaire.) Other explorers and colonialists such as Richard Kandt and Oscar Bauman were also among the Europeans who came to Rwanda in that period. However, the Rwandan kingdom had resisted both the encroachment of Arab slavers and colonial explorers, most chiefs being hostile to both, and this resistance bore witness to the unity of the Banyarwanda and the centralized government that was in place.

In the short time of its colonial rule, Germany adopted a system of indirect rule through which its authority was exercised in the already existing sociopolitical channels. The leadership of the time was through the king of Rwanda, his chiefs and their sub-chiefs, most of whom were Tutsi. The indirect rule system achieved one of its primary goals: to maintain internal peace, but it did not change the Rwandan system of government, and so did not create social tensions among the Banyarwanda.

The Belgians maintained the form of indirect rule when they took over from the Germans in 1916, but exercised their influence with far more manipulative aims. As opposed to a *laissez-faire* approach, the Belgians deliberately began a 'divide and rule' policy.

Catholics were the first among the Christian missionaries entering Rwanda, Bishop Hirth of the congregation of White Fathers being the first missionary to enter Rwanda in 1900. The White Fathers order, officially known as 'The Society of Missionaries of Our Lady of Africa', was founded in 1868 by Charles Martial A. Lavigerie. The White Fathers had tried to enter Rwanda by way of Tanzania, but failed due to a combination of illness and opposition.[2] Bishop Hirth, surrounded by porters and guards, travelled to Rwanda from Tanzania wishing to meet the Rwandan king at his residency, but the German colonial representatives were aware of his coming and had informed the Rwandan king of his arrival. Here began the triangular relationship that introduced the mission church to the indigenous leadership structures of the time. The White Fathers initiated their first strategic contact with the German colonial administrators, who in turn introduced them to the Rwandan king, this German contact making the White Fathers' entry into Rwanda relatively easy. Still, the Rwandan king expressed his resentment of an outside religion replacing the veneration and appeasement of ancestors, and although Bishop Hirth was well received by the king's entourage at the king's palace, the king himself avoided the bishop.

When the White Fathers finally established a presence in Rwanda, they were protected by the Germans. Because of their service to the Fathers, the Germans expected their respect and support of their indirect rule policy. But the French-speaking White Fathers did not necessarily cooperate with the Germans.

The Protestant Christian mission agencies arrived much later. In 1907, the Evangelische Missionsgesellschaft für Ostafrica from Germany became the first Protestant missionary effort to enter Rwanda. Their goal was to convert African people (Rwandan included) and turn them into useful Christian citizens of the German colony. Following the German missionaries who established the Presbyterian Church in Rwanda, English Anglican missionaries arrived in 1922 who has been sent by the Church Missionary Society (CMS), already active in Uganda. The arrival of the Anglican missionaries seemed to open Rwanda's door to other mission groups, including the Danish Baptist Mission and the Seventh Day Adventists in 1927.

In 1936, the Free Methodist Mission arrived. Although there are many more small mission groups that came into Rwanda after the colonial days, the last major mission agencies to enter Rwanda were the Southern Baptist Mission of America, and the Swedish Pentecostals. The extended pattern of mission agencies' entrance demonstrates the inherent resistance of Rwanda to the outside world of missionaries and colonial exploiters. Most mission agencies that came into the country had been established in neighbouring countries. There were Catholics in Uganda and in Tanzania, entering Rwanda from Tanzania, Anglicans in Uganda; Danish Baptists and Swedish missionaries in Burundi; and the Free Methodist Mission in Zaire.

These missionaries were entering a country with a complex leadership structure. Following German colonial leadership through indirect rule that utilized traditional Rwandan channels, the Belgians extended European control by removing powers from the traditional leaders, leaving them with minimal delegated responsibilities. Missionaries played it safe in their relationship with the local leaders and the colonial officials. Although they did not necessarily agree on the principles of leadership exercised, there is no question that they felt more comfortable with the colonial administrators, who also ensured their security. The German administrators and Catholic missionaries were not on the best terms, nor were the missionaries among themselves: the Catholics were often set against the Protestants, the Anglican and Catholic missionaries' history of sour relationships stemming from Uganda.

The colonial administrators and the mission leaders had different views regarding the people of Rwanda, especially Hutu and Tutsi. The traditional structure used to accomplish colonial objectives was not favoured by the Catholic missionaries, who termed it 'oppressive', while the Protestants tried to remain apolitical. Belgian colonial rule came with an ear bent toward the Catholic mission, and this added a different twist to the whole church–state relationship, leading the Rwandan people into developing invisible walls of hatred between themselves. It was, for instance, the colonial authorities and the Catholic mission church of the time that introduced the Hamitic myth, that the Tutsis were not of African origin, but of foreign descent.

As those who committed genocide in 1994 killed people and littered rivers with their bodies, their own media called on militia to move fast and finish the job, inciting them to 'send the Tutsis back to their origin' through the local rivers all the way down the river Nile. The extremist Hutus believed the teachings and writings of the early Catholic missiologists and colonial anthropologists and, sadly, to this day persist in their efforts to eliminate survivors of – and witnesses to – their holocaust.[3]

TWO

The Church Begins

MISSIONARY WORK BEGAN in Rwanda in the late nineteenth century. To understand the background and circumstances, we need to understand some of the context both in Europe and in precolonial Rwanda.

In Europe, people were enjoying relative peace and a rising prosperity which continued until the First World War. The period in which missionary work started in Rwanda is known as the 'Great Century' of Christian missions; it is also a century characterized by the expansion of European peoples and rapid exploration by man of his physical environment. As the church historian Kenneth Scott Latourette wrote, 'the impact of Europeans and their cultures brought the beginning of vast revolutions among non-European peoples'. Christianity in Europe was being endangered by intellectualism: in Great Britain intellectuals rejected Christianity, or disseminated views which shook the faith of many; in certain societies people saw inconsistencies in the Bible, and therefore declared that they could not believe in God. In spite of such threats to the faith there was a strong sense of spiritual development and vision for missions in the Church.

In Africa, European explorers, missionaries and traders were all busily engaged in exploring – and exploiting. The motivating factor of colonial expansion was the search for resources, markets, settlement, prestige and power. The gospel had been introduced in West Africa, and in East Africa, both Catholics and Protestants were evangelizing. Uganda, Kenya and Tanzania were well ahead of Rwanda on the missions schedule, the church mission coming to Rwanda 37 years after the first missionary arrived on the east coast of Africa. Missionaries were working in difficult circumstances, and were persecuted by Arab traders.

When the White Fathers arrived in Rwanda under the leadership of Bishop Hirth, their goal was to evangelize the king, his Tutsi chiefs and their entourage. It was within the White Fathers' mission strategy initially to relate and develop close relationships with traditional leaders for the purpose of introducing the gospel through them to the greater Rwandan population. In his church planting, Bishop Hirth found that he had to deal with two tiers of government: traditional Rwandan government, and the German colonial administrators, the latter, under the leadership of Von Goetzen, having promised protection for Hirth and his team. As Ian Linden expounded, 'German rule, never in reality more than a handful of soldiers and administrators, did not change the nature of the Rwanda state.'[2] It has to be noted that their indirect rule actually invigorated both the hierarchical leadership and the power of the king and his chiefs. Indirect rule meant the traditional sociopolitical structures were still intact, strong and functioning despite the German presence. The absolute leadership power of the king was respected and supported by the Germans for whatever the duration of his rule was to be; the king, his court, army and chiefs were still responsible for the affairs of the country. Even though often described by outsiders as 'complex', the traditional structure in Rwanda found by the German colonialists was effective, and although Bishop Hirth was not as impressed by the structure as the Germans were, he had to cope with their indirect rule policy.

Precolonial and German Rwanda enjoyed the unity of one people in one nation: the three groups of people who made up the Banyarwanda appreciated and complemented each other under the leadership of 'the father of the nation, Umwami' (the king). There was a common belief and saying: '*Umwamin' Umukobga ntibagira Ubwoko*' ('A king and a young woman do not belong to any tribe or have an ethnic identity'), and in Rwanda the saying made sense: a woman could be married into any ethnic society, and a king was the king for Hutu, Tutsi and Twa alike. It is only with the introduction of the colonial powers that we see a sharp distinction among the three Rwandan peoples that is based on ethnic rather than socioeconomic status. This distinction was first mentioned by the White Fathers, who complained about the Rwandan socioeconomic system. To them, the sociopolitical structure reinforced by German colonial rule reflected social injustice. The missionaries' view of the situation differed from that of the German administrators, and set them up for a 'love–hate' relationship that both sides manipulated at the expense of the Rwandan society. Both the Rwandan leadership and population close to the White Fathers took advantage of the conflict between the White Fathers and the German administrators. There is a saying in Kinyarwanda, '*Ntawiba ahetse*,' that translates 'No one steals with a baby on his back.' Why not? The baby is watching – and learning from the example. Political intrigue and manipulation seem to have been what the White Fathers and German colonial administrators taught their watching subjects.

As well as cattle-herding and farming, metal, wood, pottery, basket-making and leather work were also part of the Rwandan economy. Cash was non-existent, so the exchange of goods played a major role, and of all the elements of economy, cattle held a special position in socioeconomic exchange. Wealth was measured on the basis of how many cows one had. Alexandre Kimenyi reflected on the importance of cattle: 'Cows are not only a symbol of wealth, but they are also sacred. Only precious and beautiful things can be compared to cows, the ultimate value . . . for most people one of the goals in life is to acquire as many cows as possible.'[3] The main way of obtaining cattle was through *ubuhake*, a social hierarchical system then deeply rooted in Rwandan society. In today's terms, *ubuhake* was an employment contract, whereby an individual was given a cow or cows for his own personal use and protection in exchange for his services, and the system reached across ethnic lines. The only people who could not become a 'client' in the country were the king and a few certain people with close relationships to the king. *Ubuhake* could result in strong close relationships. I remember hearing stories from my parents of young adults who would leave their homes in search of *ubuhake* and therefore the wealth the Rwandan culture could offer. They learned a lot from the kings and the chiefs during their *ubuhake* period of contracted employment, and when the time came, they returned home with herds to impress their families and their peers. Most elderly people would equate a successful *ubuhake* to the success that could be achieved through today's educational avenues.

In general, *ubuhake* puts Hutus at a disadvantage, because their natural economic focus was on land rather than cattle, but it also weighed heavily on poor Tutsi. Client Tutsi gave cow gifts to the chiefs or their masters, and rendered services that gave them some kind of status in the society. The inconvenience of the system affected Hutu, Tutsi and Twa alike. As Tutsis took advantage of their cows, Hutu in certain parts of the country with smaller Tutsi populations developed a similar system based on land. Here the practice was mainly between Hutus, as an exchange based not on cattle, but on land.

Things changed in the early years of the Christian missions in Rwanda. The economic relationship of European churches with new converts who were largely Hutus introduced a new dynamic. The payment for services rendered by Hutu converts to the White Fathers introduced to the economy a new exchange based on new products, many of them imported to Rwanda. The situation was made worse by the introduction of Asian traders brought into the country by German administrators. The new sources of income introduced by the colonialists, missionaries and Asian merchants were soon to start a process that undermined *ubuhake* and the Tutsi chiefs' order of authority. The White Fathers on their mission station provided, in a sense, a new system of *ubuhake*, biased toward the Hutu side, whom the White Fathers viewed as the oppressed people of the society. Simultaneously, the German administrators and leadership as a whole favoured the Tutsi for their effective leadership, and respected the traditional structures out of a desire to maintain peace. There was also growing competition for the labour the average Rwandan could provide: German administrators needed labourers, as did missionaries and Rwandan nobles. Paul Hiebert is right when he states that 'leadership, power, control and manipulation are aspects of all groups and societies'.[4]

Both colonialists and colonial missionaries found in Rwanda a nation with a common belief in a supreme being. Though not given to a cult of worship, Rwandans – Tutsi, Hutu and Twa alike – believed in a God who created, and who demonstrated the attributes of a living being: intelligence, power, a will and emotion. They viewed him as the God of Rwanda. God's name is a part of the day-to-day vocabulary of an average Rwandan. The Banyarwanda named (and still name) their children in recognition of God's attributes and activities in relation to the people he created. God's grace, love, kindness and power are depicted in Rwandan names, proverbs and legends. Though invisible, he is believed to be always present. Kimenyi has expressed that '... with the advent of Christianity, however, names referring to Imana have increased: Nsengimana "I pray God," Nsengiyumva "I pray to the one who listens," Habimana "God exists." '[5] In the 1994 relief operations, it was not uncommon to hear words such as '*Habaye ah'Imana*' ('It was only God's will') or '*Imana yakinze Ukuboko*' ('God protected with His hand') from both Christian and non-Christian survivors of the genocide.

The Banyarwanda were more concerned by the ancestral spirits, generally believed to be malevolent everyday influences. Appeasement of ancestors was, and in certain places still is, practised. Rwandans therefore believe in life after death.

The Rwandan people, especially the nobles, resisted change in religion. The first missionaries' intent, you will remember, was to evangelize through the king and his chiefs. Bishop Hirth's demand for land near the king's palace to accomplish that goal was denied, so the evangelism that was to have begun with the king and his chiefs was limited to the peasants, who later converted in great numbers. It is here that the Church became known as 'the Hutu church', later empowered with an educated native clergy who by the 1940s were working hard to challenge *ubuhake*. Because the White Fathers held one view of the situation in Rwanda favouring the Hutu, while the Germans held the other in support of traditional structures, the relationship between the German administrators and the White Fathers went from bad to worse, and they drew Rwandan allies on both sides. (We should note here that certain White Fathers were of the same view as the German administrators, but that the majority view held sway in the order.) Even though the White Fathers advocated change, and their evangelistic approach was rejected by the nobles, they did not give up but continued to make contacts, this time with the help of Hutu converts. Their persistence paid off, as we will see in the chapters to come.

There were advantages and disadvantages to the relationships developed by both the colonial masters and the White Fathers. The White Fathers' relationship with the peasants and nobles opened doors for evangelism and Christian ministry, and changed the standards of life for some. The clear disadvantage was the creation of a strained relationship between the Tutsis and the Hutu by preferring one group over the other. Christian love does not discriminate under any circumstances; the White Fathers, it seems, should have been under an obligation to bridge the divide as Christ would have done. However, the German administrators and Catholic missionaries alike favoured one group against the other and the result was a widening of the divisions they had already introduced.

The coming of the Protestant Church to the country added an interesting ingredient to the relationships discussed above. King Musinga knew and saw what was coming, and made an interesting decision. The relationship between the German administrators and the White Fathers had gone sour to the point where the Germans forced a non-expansion strategy on the Catholic Church. When a Lutheran missionary, Pastor Johansen arrived to be introduced, King Musinga warmly welcomed him and gave him a place only a few hours' walk from the king's palace to conduct Bible studies. Musinga's intention was to take advantage of the competitive situation. Musinga saw both Protestants and Catholics as preaching the same doctrine, but to the Catholic Bishop Classe, the similarity of Catholic doctrine to Protestant was like the similarity of a Hutu to a Tutsi.

Throughout the period of first German and then Belgian rule, traditional institutions and social structures remained unchallenged until 1926. It is at this time that reforms determined to bring change to the traditional institutions began, and the Church played a significant role. The arrival of

the White Fathers at the king's court 6 years after the arrival of the first
German colonial master was probably not perceived by the Rwandan king's
court as an evangelistic effort, but as the arrival of more European white
colonial masters. When the time came for Bishop Hirth to be given land to
build his first station, he was given a site about 50 kilometres south of the
king's court and residency. This was a profound disappointment to the
bishop, whose hope had been fixed on establishing a church mission station
at the king's capital to house a non-religious school for the children of the
chiefs. In spite of this obstacle – which may have been a blessing in disguise
– the White Fathers kept their zeal for religious activities in Rwanda,
penetrated the society and got to know the people and their culture.

The German administration had expected respect from the White
Fathers, but the Fathers seemed to act on their own; and after the White
Fathers failed to secure a place near the Rwandan king's palace, Bishop
Hirth opted for popular mass evangelism and, later, church planting, the
majority of his converts being peasant Hutus. But he did not give up the
idea of aggressively pursuing the king and his chiefs; both the German
administrators and Bishop Hirth wanted to work through the existing
structures, albeit for two different purposes. For the German administrators it was for the maintenance of peace and harmony in the nation. For
Bishop Hirth, it was a question of fulfilling the strategy given him by
Cardinal Lavigerie to evangelize through the chiefs. Reaching the king and
his chiefs would have facilitated a 'change agent' strategy toward mass
evangelism.

The early German and Belgian emphases on indirect rule gave power for
a while to the traditional sociopolitical structures. Further, the idea of
school for the children of chiefs and the preference to evangelize through
the traditional structures favoured the people of the regime. By 1919 the
Belgians had deepened ethnic divisions, producing much of the bitterness
that has continued until today. Knowingly or not, the colonial administrators and the White Fathers had advanced the Tutsi at the expense of the
Hutu.

In concluding this chapter, it is important to point out that although for
several years Tutsi nobles used the system of *ubuhake*, that fact alone does
not prove that ethnic inequalities in precolonial Rwanda existed as people
have been led to believe. The system affected both Hutu and Tutsi, and was
an issue of personal wealth. Both Tutsi and Hutu accepted *ubuhake* as a
part of their social life. The problem came when outsiders, with pre-
conceptions of Rwandan relationships, took advantage of the system to

divide and rule. First, indirect rule formalized the system and gave it a political power twist different from what the Rwandan people had ever experienced. The favouritism shown by both the colonial rulers and the missionaries imposed solid and high walls between the two major groups of the Banyarwandese. To consider such a division as ethnic, though, violates the observations of those such as Bishop Classe, who stated, 'the term "Tutsi" often refers not to origin but social condition, or wealth, especially as regards cattle: whoever is a chief, or is rich will often be referred to as "Tutsi." Frequently, also, because of their manner or their language.'[6] Every foreign group to come would choose sides between Rwandans, making the conflict more visible and obvious in the colonial Rwandan church. Nowhere in the history of precolonial Rwanda had there been war between the two groups: wars were against other nations, or kingdoms, but not among the Rwandan people. The problems between the White Fathers and the Germans set the stage for taking sides, and for the ongoing attempt to manipulate those sides one against the other. Following the fall of German rule to the Belgians, the indirect rule system employed by the Germans was doomed to fail. The French-speaking White Fathers and the Belgian administrators established strong relationships that made the new administrators depend heavily on the missionaries. The White Fathers had learned the culture, the language, and held power in the areas of their mission stations. History shows that the Catholic missionaries and their Belgian administrator friends were the architects of the scheme that has severely disrupted the coexistence of the Rwandan people.

The mission work in Rwanda that we are about to examine in the next chapter clarifies even more for us the initial decisive role of the Roman Catholic Church in the sociopolitical ideology that has left the country widely divided even today.

THREE

Early Fruits of the Hard Labour

THE RESULTS OF the early missionary work were phenomenal. The Rwandan people quickly opened their minds and souls to the gospel, regardless of the methods of delivery and factors that might have influenced the openness and receptivity of the new religion. Roman Catholics were the pioneers of the Christian mission work in Rwanda, the Protestant Church coming much later. We will consider them in historical order.

The Catholic mission's approach that was initially rejected by the king and his nobles was the strategy the White Fathers' mission executive and founder Cardinal Lavigerie had recommended. He had challenged his missionaries to reach the soul and spirit of the leaders first, and then to evangelize the rest of the population through them. In fact, he hoped for a mass following once the leaders were converted. Lavigerie reflected, 'in a violent society of multiple tribes under a patriarchal regime, the most important thing is to win the heart of leaders'.[1] When this approach failed, the White Fathers were forced to start with the most accommodating group of people in the country. The 'begin with the leaders' strategy was reversed, with encouraging results among the poor Hutus and impoverished lower-class Tutsis; the peasants of the village of Save formed the base of the first mission. For about 20 years, the Tutsis kept distant while Hutus were converting in great numbers. The White Fathers enjoyed their success, writing many letters back to their mission leader and friends expressing the unbelievably profitable results of their hard work. Later, some Tutsis realized the sociopolitical implications of a large number of Hutus converting to Christianity and started softening to the missionaries' approach. According to my interview with His Majesty King Kigeri V, now residing in Washington, DC, King Musinga was opposed to the new religion; he not only felt that the new religion was supplanting the Rwandan traditional religion that recognized God, but also feared losing his power and authority. He was deeply concerned that he would no longer recognize his people, since the priests were baptizing them and giving them new non-Kinyarwandan names.[2] In general, the missionaries were perceived less as gospel preachers and church planters than as European colonialists whose goal and objectives were to conquer the country and assume leadership. As Adrian Hastings wrote, 'Clearly the churches came to most parts of the continent within the wider context of colonial expansion: the two movements were often closely linked.'[3]

Numerous requests continued to be made for a mission to be established near the king's court, but the king and his chiefs persisted. Approval would have implied the king's consent to the new religion, the after-effect probably being mass conversion such as the missionaries expected from their original strategy. Resistance to Catholic missionaries was gradually implanted among certain people of influence in the Rwandan population to try to control the spread of their work. Passive opposition later developed into some limited violent resistance, and even the first year of missionary work in Rwanda was not without violence, mission stations being broken into and the houses of new converts burned. To the majority of Rwandan people, the new converts were at worst traitors, and at best unwise for their decisions. Most lived at the mission stations, humiliated and basically considered non-human in their native community. They struggled with both the external and internal conflicts between the old ways of life and their newly adopted biblical and Western values; the missionaries' low view of the Rwandan culture, combined with a heavy dose of Western theology and a colonial mentality, further confused the situation.

The purpose of the new converts' isolation was their training, protection and preparation to recruit new followers. Further, Rwandan converts provided labour while learning skills that came to be profitable later in life. To the missionaries, the conflicts and persecution experienced by the new converts were news and signs of hardships to be communicated in 'prayer letters' back to their European support base.

The missionaries' efforts to learn about Rwanda were crucial for their success. Not only did they immediately embark on the task of evangelism and mission station building, but they also learned the language, customs, beliefs and the sociopolitical structures of the country. The White Fathers themselves, as well as the objects in their possession, became an attraction in the Rwandan community. These pioneer missionaries acquired their field missionary 'basic training' from the alarmed Rwandan people who spent hours looking at the strangers. The quickly acquired knowledge gave the missionaries confidence and an open door to evangelize and Westernize the Rwandan people.

Although the location of the land was not what they had desired, the very fact that the White Fathers acquired land for mission stations helped to establish them quickly and successfully in Rwanda. The first two were founded in the most highly populated and easily accessed regions of the country; five were founded within 4 years of the missionaries' arrival in three parts of the country, with two stations in the north, two in the south and one in the east. After a few years of trying hard, the White Fathers also successfully acquired land and established a station in an area not far from the capital. The evolution of their work, and their influence in the community, worried the king, so that the German administration had to 'pull strings' in order for the White Fathers to expand further after they had built their fifth mission. Although this act of intervention confused the king, he acceded to the request, but did not hide his fear of losing power in favour of the Catholic missionaries. With five stations already, they seemed to the king to be everywhere. He wondered aloud where the colonialists and missionaries wanted him to go.[4]

The secret behind reaching their first followers was that the missionaries took advantage of socioeconomic inequalities. They labelled the Rwandan system as 'social injustice', reached out to the mainly Hutu lower class and gradually moved their efforts up the ladder to the common people. This is one reason why friction in years to come would be identified as being between the Hutus and a Tutsi-dominated society. Cardinal Lavigerie's philosophy of missions had emphasized charitable work geared to improving the socioeconomic lives of people, with education as a key tool toward that end. But while the instruction was that souls be redeemed first, and action regarding the physical and social concerns of humans come second, the winning of souls through proselytizing was not executed in Rwanda as Lavigerie would have wished; the White Fathers' first emphasis being on the socioeconomic development of the disadvantaged.

The missionary influence spread through medical work, schools, social assistance and in-kind payments for services rendered. Handouts of clothing, salt, pins and other imported objects attracted people to the stations. Obviously, the missionaries took advantage of the sociopolitical economic situation in the country. As Rwandans associated the material possession of new goods in their communities with the missionaries, the poor and the sick became advocates of this new relationship, life at the mission stations and, in some cases, conversion. The converts started enjoying all kinds of benefits, including protection. 'Becoming a Christian could bring considerable material advantages; essentially it brought one within the modern, progressive sector of society – the sector with paid jobs such as teacher, clerk or lawyer.'[5]

The mission station environment combined with the personal influence of the missionaries to create a whole new lifestyle for the converts. The missionaries' declared goal was to help people out of their misery, and it is important to be reminded here that to the White Fathers, *ubuhake* was a great social injustice. *Ubuhake* also kept the perceived wealth in Rwanda away from the majority of the population, and so was viewed as oppressive in nature. Is it not then amazing that colonialism was not viewed as oppressive, nor its injustices addressed by the same missionaries? Although it was a thoroughly oppressive system that raped most colonized nations of their wealth and resources, who dared address it? Colonial missionaries were therefore often viewed by Rwandans as agents of exploitation and of the expansion of colonial powers. To this day they are viewed as people who pacified Rwandans even as they occupied their lands. As K. P. Yohannan wrote, 'The gospel and its proclamation by white foreigners are portrayed as a sinister form of imperialism. Christian missions are usually linked to every injustice or sinful exploitation of native peoples during the colonial era.'[6] If the missionary intent was to help people out of their misery, the Rwandan people as a whole should have been helped out of colonialism, but the missionaries' message to the targeted audience contained convincing elements. The population had watched the poor peoples' lives improving, the sick being healed and all being materially blessed from missionary handouts.

Short-term missionaries became new patrons in the community with a different type of *ubuhake*, here based on imported goods being exchanged for services from the converts. These missionaries also offered protection to the converts from the demands of the ruling class, and the work of the colonial master. Both the traditional sociopolitical structure and colonial exploitation played motivational roles in the Rwandan response to both the Catholic and Protestant church mission endeavours. I believe that the Spirit of God convinced many to conversion, but I also will not hesitate to say that social, material, political and other personal motives encouraged the tremendous response to Christianity, irrespective of a heartfelt commitment. In the camp where I spent my childhood, I remember my family and hundreds of other refugees going to church solely for what was to be distributed afterwards. Slowly, many would be converted to Christianity even though originally their main aim was to receive this material assistance. Others stayed away from church after the church relief programme was discontinued. Materialism showed itself at both ends of this relationship, of course, and some missionaries in the relief distributions would go as far as stating, 'There will be clothing distributions for those who have made a decision for Christ.'

Elderly Rwandans say that those who were involved in some way with the mission stations were exempted from the forced labour demanded by either the chiefs or the colonial administrators. By 1907, the mission stations were widely accessible to the Rwandan people, and many wanted to 'convert' in order to get jobs or material goods. Many became Christians; some, catechists. The early Rwandan movement toward Christianity was not necessarily a serious decision for many, or born from a love for the Lord as was reported in missionary letters and reports back to individual or church sponsors. Many Rwandans who professed to be Christians, privately still practised the traditional ancestral worship, and a lack of both proper teaching and discipleship among converts became a major issue and contributed to ignorance about their newly adopted religious life. The result was that it was simply confusing for Rwandans to apply Christianity to their everyday culture.

What is to count in the missions? Quantity or quality? Sometimes quality comes out of quantity, but there is a danger of looking at Christianity in terms of quantity rather than quality. Relationships cannot be quantified, but as human beings we tend to look at the 'numbers of Christians' and assume all is well rather than analysing the true relationship of a people with their maker. A painful example of the danger of trusting quantity is that of the recent situation in Rwanda, believed to be 86 per cent 'Christian'. How, in such a 'Christian' country, could so much genocidal blood flood the church sanctuaries? It is ironic that Rwanda is also where the well-known East African Revival, that swept Central and East Africa, started. Did Christianity in Rwanda dig deep down in the hearts of Rwandan people, or was it just an association and affiliation with the Church that might have originated from adherents that were attracted by socioeconomic and political gains? Hastings is right in stating, 'The church could not possibly remain uninvolved in the spate of political conflicts which have swept across Africa – their members are fully caught up in them and generally on more than one side.'[7]

Even though mass evangelism was powerful and strongly moving among the Hutus, the White Fathers' desire to reach the Tutsi leadership was still a spiritual burden. The chiefs finally showed interest in the new religion; with the king's conversion, a new door opened for the ruling class since now Christianity added to their already respected status. And so ended resistance to the Catholic missionaries. Education and employment influenced the newfound openness in the ruling class, especially since the Belgians were preferring the educated for political office under their patronage; and it was not long before the Catholic Church favoured the Tutsi ruling class for education and employment. This favouritism, and its closeness and involvement with the colonial administrators, virtually married the Catholic Church to the state, such that under the leadership of Bishop Classe, it became a state church with a strong influence in matters of civil government.

The spirit of division was spreading. The different views held by both of Rwanda's colonial masters, first Germany and later Belgium, had become known to the majority of the new Christian community in Rwanda and their key community leaders. As we have seen, German colonial leaders viewed the Tutsis as efficient leaders, while the Catholic missionaries (and later the Belgian colonial leaders) viewed them as oppressors. Despite the resistance encountered at the leadership level and differences in socio-political views with the German colonial officials, the Catholic Church experienced an enormous growth among the peasant Hutus. Their hard work resulted in the building of mission stations and branches (sub-stations) within walking distance of each other. The White Fathers became what Henry Venn calls 'station' missionaries. As he puts it, 'the missionary whose labours are blest to the gathering in of converts, naturally desires to keep his converts under his own charge, to minister to them as a pastor and to rule them as native congregation'.[8]

The numerical growth of the Church among the Hutus was astounding; while Hutu believers were growing in number around the Catholic mission stations from the early 1900s, the conversion of Tutsis and especially those in the ruling class was not at all widespread until the 1920s. The conversion of the king and nobles broke the ties of royalty to the traditional religion, which the king and his court had previously wished to preserve. Even with inroads to Rwandan rulers, the missionaries continued to proselytize among the Hutus, as until this time, the Catholic Church in Rwanda had been basically a Hutu church. But for the Catholics, the king's conversion to Catholicism was a major success that gave the Church a certain status in which they took pride. The conversion of the king and his chiefs, in a sense, marked an official recognition of the Catholic Church's influence in the colonial era.

Even though the Catholics experienced growth under the German rule in Rwanda, it was a slow growth as compared to that under the Belgian colonial authority. The Belgians gave special favour to the Catholic missionaries, as Belgium was a Catholic country. Financial and material support to the Church from the Belgian government enabled them to expand their many different mission activities, especially in education and medicine. This exclusive assistance continued until the 1950s.

One could summarize the factors that favoured the numerical growth of the Catholic Church as follows:

- the missionaries' reconciliation role between the Belgian colonial powers and the local authorities;
- the moral, financial and material support provided by the Belgian government;
- the conversion of the king and some of his chiefs;
- the educational institutions.

The case in Rwanda is reflected in Linden's statement: 'For many, Catholicism has simply become the religion of the powerful, an opinion for which there was ample evidence in Rwanda.'[9]

The establishment of schools, medical facilities and other missionary activities attracted more people to the church stations and to the church services. During Belgian colonial rule, the Catholic Church controlled all the schools in the country, but only Tutsis were given sufficient education to become administrators. This also brought a change in how Rwandan people got their wealth. It was no longer through *ubuhake*, but education. Bureaucracy started delegating authority to people based on their education, and thus introduced a new citizen status in Rwanda.

The Roman Catholic Church in Rwanda quickly interjected itself into political life. From the beginning, it has never been seen to rise above its switching of allegiance from one group to another – first from the Hutus to the Tutsi and later back to the Hutus. This flexibility has always presented a paradox to the Rwandan people. Somehow the Roman Catholic Church has always seemed to be able to read signs of political changes to come, and made statements that would help it either to be on neutral ground or to line up with the strong. As well expressed in *Rwanda: Death, Despair and Defiance*, 'The legacy of this identification lives on and has contributed enormously to the deep politicization of the church.'[10] As noted before, the Belgian administration collaborated with the Catholic missionaries, who had established themselves with a knowledge of both the language and the culture of the people. When the Belgian colonial rulers entered Rwanda with no knowledge of the Kinyarwanda language or of the country itself, they sought help from the missionaries with whom they shared a common language. This close and constant collaboration between colonial rulers and missionaries was a turning-point toward the European acculturation of Rwanda.

The Catholic missionaries were not necessarily in favour of King Yuhi V Musinga (r. 1897–1931), who with his chiefs had managed to keep the Rwandan people away from European cultural influence. The relationship and collaboration between the Catholic missionaries and colonial administrators made the Rwandan nobles uncomfortable and frightened their leadership. Strangely, this collaboration caused the Rwandan rulers to move towards the missionaries' intention for them. It was not long before the traditional leadership realized that the colonial administrators had moved to capture their authority. Musinga and his chiefs felt there was no possible way to stand against them. Since the Catholic Church had gained a great number of followers, and the White Fathers' influence had obviously gone too far to be stopped, the traditional leaders and their relatives moved to seize the opportunity and benefits offered by the Church before it was too late, and as a result, many chiefs began to attend church. They sent their children to school and went to catechism classes. It was at this time, predictably, that the Rwanda Catholic missionary church experienced mass conversion of chiefs, their clans and those who were protected by them.

It was not long before the colonial rulers offered employment and required that such leadership come from the newly educated Rwanda population, thus changing the traditional way of getting into leadership. Christianity and its social services brought a new criterion for social status in the country, a new requirement for leadership, and new divisions in Rwandan society. The divisions were accentuated by both religion and education. The new converts of both noble and common descent joined the educated young chiefs and sub-chiefs against the non-converted ruling class. The missionaries' influence through the converts, with full support of the Belgian administrators, resulted in the overthrow of the old nobles – including Musinga – who were considered pagans. The missionaries solidified their political power through a number of diverse reforms and actions of collaboration with the administrators, and within a short time the Belgians, not the traditional Rwandan rulers, were responsible for the nomination of chiefs and sub-chiefs and for the removal of many of the king's powers.

The initial intention of the Belgians was to maintain the German approach of indirect rule, but in the Belgian Congo (now Zaire), Belgian administrators had become used to giving direction and taking the affairs of the country into their own hands. Uncomfortable with indirect rule, they decided to govern Rwanda as they did the Congo. First, they removed the power of the king to order capital punishment, then they imposed regulations under which the king was to appoint chiefs subject to their final approval. The relationship between the Belgians and the king deteriorated to the point where the Belgians decided to remove him, replacing Musinga with his son Rudahigwa (r. 1931–59). For a foreigner to involve himself in the traditional affairs and the innermost secrets of the Rwanda kings was unheard of, but the logic behind the Belgian rule was that if the chiefs were the representatives of the king, they were also representatives of the colonial administration. Indirect rule was no more; instead the chiefs, sub-chiefs and even the king were all subordinates of colonial rule and this did nothing short of establishing colonial authority over the population as a whole. Unfortunately, by buying into the Catholic power structure, the Belgians had gained power by favouring one group against the other, thus contributing to the creation of conflict between the two major groups of Rwandan society.

In *Mission in Rwanda*, G. Logiest suggests that the importance of religious missions in the sociopolitical context of Rwanda cannot be emphasized enough: 'The Catholic Church in Rwanda grew into a type of first estate which both nobles and Belgians had to accommodate.'[11] The Catholic Church, as well as the mainline Protestant denominations that followed, would have done better to avoid close identification and involvement with politics in order not to compromise their Christian witness.

After some initial vacillation the Belgians attempted to impose a uniform policy on Rwanda, to rule through a reformed nobility and to educate a bureaucracy. As educational attainment became the key to political office under Belgian patronage, the Tutsi strategy of keeping the missionaries at arm's length was abandoned.

The Protestant Church in Rwanda came into the picture much later, the first Protestant missionary arriving 7 years after the Catholic missionaries had been established. Their arrival in 1907, in the form of Presbyterian missionaries from Germany, shook the Catholics, who described the newcomers as 'false teachers'. But using the same evangelistic and mission establishment strategy as the Catholics, Protestants often preceded their teachings with distributions of clothing, soap and salt. The Protestant mission suffered a great blow with the departure of the German administrators. Belgians, with their Catholic background, favoured the White

Fathers' mission work over the Protestant effort. In fact, there was little in terms of Protestant church mission activities until the late 1920s. Among the early arrivals were the Anglicans, in 1922: Doctor Stanley Smith and Reverend Geoffrey Holmes (sent by the Church Missionary Society) and Kossia Shalita, a Rwandan who came with them from Uganda. They established in Gahini and there they started the first Anglican mission church, now known as 'Eglise Episcopale Au Rwanda'. Before the planting and actual start of mission activities, the local leadership of Gahini made sure that the new strangers were introduced to King Musinga to explain about their mission and envisioned work.

The burning desire of the Anglicans was to proclaim Christ through evangelism. The Anglican missionaries had previously made an attempt to come to Rwanda, their main obstacle at that time being the Catholic missionaries, who feared the Protestant mission as a whole. In my relief programme visits immediately after the takeover by the Rwandan Patriotic Front (RPF) government, I was privileged to visit Gahini, where I met Mrs Majoro, one of the people familiar with the Gahini story. With her were a number of old men who experienced not only the 'touching of Jesus' feet at the Gahini hill', but also the start of the Gahini church mission station. As they were taking me around, to find a place to build a home for unaccompanied children, they would tell me the stories behind the old buildings and the mission station as a whole. They remarked that the first Anglican missionaries were wonderful, courageous men. Names such as Stanley Smith, Geoffrey Holmes and Joe Church were often mentioned. Their initial involvement in the church planting, establishment of schools, medical work and literature actually enhanced their relationships with people in the community. They were known for their tireless relief work during the famine years, and their choice to be apolitical. The Anglican missionaries were doing a wonderful work that King Musinga often described as exemplary. Gahini became the favourite mission station of King Musinga, who during one of his visits offered them a drum called 'Rwamu', to be played only at Christmas or during the king's visits. In the 1960s, after the fall of the Rwanda kingdom to the then-President Kayibanda, Dr Joe Church refused to play the 'Rwamu' at Kayibanda's visit. His rationale was that since the drum was used to play for Christ, the king of all nations and all people, it could not be played for a ruler who discriminated against people because of their ethnicity as did Kayibanda.

In 1936, Gahini experienced an 'unusual visit of the Holy Spirit', as it was put to me by the old men at Gahini, the greatest result of the Christian mission work in the country. A movement recognized by all to be an extraordinary work of the Holy Spirit in the lives of God's people, the Rwanda Revival is actually attributed (by those with firsthand experience of it) to a return to Bible study and prayer by the Christians in Gahini, and arose out of a deep sense of personal need for both the nationals and the missionaries.

It was also in 1936 that the Belgian colonial administrators introduced a national identification card based on ethnic distinction. Dr Smith and his mission organization colleagues opposed the issuing of the cards and encouraged church followers not to accept them. Dr Smith did not stop there, but also worked to request an open-school policy for all Rwandan children, and in 1949, Protestant children were finally given a place in what was largely a Catholic institution, the majority of whose students were children from noble families. Schools, hospitals, literature and agricultural programmes have been major emphases of the Protestant mission church through the years. Many of their early missionaries were doctors and educators with a burden for the establishment of churches, schools and medical institutions.

The Catholic and Protestant missions were rivals in search of the support and favour of the Tutsi authorities in power. Knowing the power the Catholic Church had and the support it enjoyed with the colonial rule, most chiefs, sub-chiefs and even the king converted to Catholicism. According to Logiest, when the Catholics later changed their politics and dropped their support of the Tutsi hierarchy, the Protestant churches rushed to fill the void. Logiest, one of the administrators, admits having difficulties with the Protestant leaning.[12]

The colonial powers succeeded in separating Rwandan people by emphasizing individual identities and then ascribing social values to each of the two groups, thus placing an invisible wall of hatred between them. The Catholic missionaries echoed and in fact practised the same discriminatory behaviour prior to the Belgian rule. The whole colonial administration and the work and social services rendered by missionaries focused on distinctions between the two major ethnic groups. The most recent genocide in Rwanda derives in part from deep historic divisions in Rwandan society created by the colonial rulers and the churches. Acknowledging that there were class stratifications in precolonial Rwanda, the colonial rulers brought it about that they were perceived as ethnic divisions.

Historically, the influence of the Protestant churches on politics in Rwanda has been less pronounced, mainly because of their smaller size and lack of unity. Protestant leaders tended not to criticize the inequalities of prerevolutionary society as did some Catholics. Before the colonial rule, especially that of the Belgians with the Catholic Church, the distinctions between Hutus and Tutsis were not rigid. This rigidity came as a result of first, educating children only of the chiefs, and second, favouring the Hutus when the Tutsis rejected or kept Christianity at a distance. At first, Protestant missionaries avoided involvement in politics. In the 1959 massacres of the Tutsi, however, Protestant missionaries of the Anglican church wrote to protest. Dr Joe Church recalls, 'We protested in two memoranda our non-participation in politics as a mission but our stations became places of refuge for those who were being hunted and killed.'[13]

Manipulation of the Rwandan people into political entities started with the colonial administrations. The Church seems to have played a dual mission: that of converting the heathen to Christianity, and that of contributing to the colonial administration by way of Western cultural influence. It is dangerous for the Church to take sides in politics, more so when Christian teachings are organized to fit a political ideology. The early mission church in Rwanda chose to identify herself closely with the colonial power and engaged in a struggle for Hutu liberation that came to be clearly expressed in the late 1950s. There was a strong desire to change the traditional sociopolitical structure and abolish *ubuhake*, and the Church took the lead in a role it should have left to the colonial administrators. It is interesting that the colonial administrators very much depended upon the missionaries whenever it was time for major decisions. Thus it was the Catholic Church that influenced the Belgian administration to switch its allegiance away from the Tutsis, making possible a transfer of power to Hutus.

Each in his own sphere of influence, the missionary and the colonial administrator were agents of the same system. The result? The Church, especially in its Catholic expression, had from the early 1930s become the portal of authority in Rwanda, after the conversion of the king and his followers.

Part Two

—

Conversion to the Faith –
and to the Fashion

FOUR

The Christian Faith and European Customs

BOTH THE MISSIONARIES and the colonial administrators came as agents of change even though they may have had different results in mind. Colonial governments gave significant moral support, help and encouragement to the missionaries' undertakings, thus helping bring about and speed changes that were not exclusively spiritual in nature. Throughout the history of missions, missionaries have been agents of social change whether they intended to be or not.

Biblically, the gospel of Jesus Christ is not tied to any one's individual culture group. But quite often the missionaries were unaware of what was biblical or the influence of their own ecclesiastical upbringing and cultural values. Unfortunately for the Rwandan culture, the 'good news bearers' embarked upon their mission viewing Rwanda through their own cultural contact lenses. Having lived in several cultures, let me acknowledge the fact that this is truly a difficult obstacle, and therefore a problem to any cross-cultural missionary. The major difference today, however, is the value given to the indigenous people's culture in missions. Contrast this with the way early missionaries viewed cultures of the so-called 'heathen societies', as Rwanda was considered. From my missiological training and influences, I have come to an understanding and belief – along with the overwhelming majority of my colleagues – that our view of Scripture and our view of culture affect our approach to evangelism, discipleship and mission strategy.

There is a saying in the Rwandan culture that 'truth is often communicated through joking'. When Rwandan people say jokingly '*Kirizia ya kuye kirazira*,' meaning that 'the Church removed taboos,' this not only communicates the Church's removal of some native taboos and breaking of other cultural traditions, but also the fact that Christian beliefs have replaced them. Turning to God and to Christianity as a new religion brought a new value system that produced noticeable changes in the lives of people. Without going into deep theological discussion, we could then define and explain conversion as *a change in which a person's belief and life is redirected, and loyalties shifted and as affecting one's values by the fact that it affects one's beliefs.* In the most current language of evangelical belief, conversion is entering a new life; it is 'becoming a Christian'. As people were converted and taught Christian beliefs, they also informally learned foreign customs and quickly adopted an alien culture. Through the lenses of the missionaries and colonial administrators, the Rwandan culture was primitive and had to be civilized. Therefore, Rwandan culture and its practices were in most cases seen as a major hindrance to the gospel instead of a potential enrichment. As the influence of Western culture grew, it became, in the eyes of Rwandans, indistinguishable from Christianity.

The colonial mission church experienced a striking response among Rwandans, having made a significant contribution to the availability of social services and to the overall development of the country. Two immediate (and remarkable) changes the advent of Western Christianity brought to Rwanda were dress styles and the introduction of second names, thus creating a first and last name system that was previously non-existent in Rwanda culture. Today most educated Rwandans, or those with a strong mission church influence, have adopted the idea of the common family surname. Such Western influence came through the converts who formed excluded Christian communities around the mission stations. The Christian names introduced were of Western origin and therefore with little meaning to Rwandans, who traditionally named their children according to circumstances, events of birth, or beliefs of parents. My own parents could not even pronounce the French name 'Laurent', given to me by a Catholic priest at my infant baptism.

As Christianity took root, the influence of Christian beliefs and teaching did start reflecting in the people's understanding of God's attributes and character, resulting in a different attitude and worship approach. But conversion to Christianity meant not only change of heart for those who understood the biblical message of salvation, but also change of a whole lifestyle and therefore physical appearance. I remember missionaries and influential Christian nationals who, before the era of national pastors, would take new converts, 'clean them up', shave their hair, burn their beads and provide them with secondhand Western clothing brought by missionaries. Depending on the missionaries' theological beliefs surrounding one's security of salvation, the new converts might not be allowed back to their community for a while so that they wouldn't backslide. Becoming Christian also meant abandoning one's traditional beliefs and social practices to fit the missionaries' understanding of 'a civilized Christian'. I remember dealing with missionaries who would challenge certain traditional practices, labelling them 'non-Christian' and 'devilish', and therefore unacceptable to faithful Christians and the Church. Not only did early colonial missionaries teach Christian faith to their converts, but they also imposed Christian standards and expectations. Salvation by grace was not enough for the mission that emphasized a 'turning to God' conversion; a person had to be closely observed to see if she fitted within the prescribed pattern for a Christian.

Mission churches differ in their definition of a Christian. To use Paul Hiebert's term, missionaries and later the first converts used 'the bounded set' approach to define who was a Christian and who was not. In 'the bounded set', missionaries drew lines around their convictions, shaped by their Christian and cultural worldviews. Both worldviews had no sensitivity to Rwandan culture and traditional values, and therefore saw nothing in them worthy to be preserved (although thankfully, this narrow vision in missions has changed in recent years). The missionaries instead wanted to help people turn to both God and Western ways of life by turning away from their traditional beliefs and cultural practices in the name of 'civilization'.

Faced with questions from their new converts and national church membership, missionaries did not know how to solve their converts' dilemma surrounding the application of Christianity to culture. Instead, they provided quick answers that did not consider the context of the missionaries' new living environment and place of ministry. Those answers simply substituted foreign for traditional cultural practices. Paul's teaching, and reports of his missionary endeavours, were not of much help to either the colonial or post-colonial missionaries. In his church planting mission strategy, the apostle Paul did not try to solve problems for new converts, but emphasized that they were to exercise their Christian responsibility to work out biblical answers to their own questions. In contrast, colonial and post-colonial missionaries in Rwanda wanted their converts to be like the Christians back in their homelands.

As I have shared stories of my travels and association with missionaries with older national Christians, I have found that missionary attitudes were frequently a source of humour among them. I remember sharing with an older pastor friend (a man I highly respected) my story of how I felt missionaries were treating me. He laughed and said that I needed to know how to relate and work with them. His advice was simple: 'Listen to the missionaries, do what they want, never compromise your Christian stand and leave them alone.' He did not believe that the missionaries could be helped to understand anything but their own cultural beliefs and standards of life. 'They seem to think they know everything, even our culture,' he said to me. He was right in his observation. Many missionaries insisted that things be done their way or else one would be out of their favour. It was a situation which most national pastors and church leaders hated to experience: challenging missionaries' thinking was like going against God's will; but not challenging their thinking, when it needed to be, led people to behave, act and think like children. Those who dared challenge missionaries were sometimes considered not spiritual enough, insubordinate or unteachable. I know from personal experience. But my relationship with missionaries turned around in my favour when they realized that I did not need them. Rather then being perceived as insubordinate, not spiritual enough and unteachable, they began to see me as someone of great faith, a hard worker, and an open person. Many started treating and dealing with me at a different level. Today some of them are close friends of mine. But historically, the missionaries and colonial administrators' relationship to nationals made the nationals retreat and relate outside their convictions in order to survive.

Basically, I felt my relationship with the missionaries to be that of a child to a father. Now that I have lived in the West, where a child–father relationship has a sense of respect, love and desire to build confidence and self-esteem in the child, I don't believe that was the nature of my relationship with the missionaries of my childhood and youth. There is a sense in which I felt they wanted me to learn their ways of behaving and to appropriate their convictions rather than developing my own. They were also quick to make decisions for me in situations where they let their children make their own decisions. Although the Christian value of any cultural practice not understood by them was quickly questioned, many of their own practices were not understood in the Rwandan context, but never questioned. Instead, we were all led to conclude that they were Christian practices when in fact they were more cultural and denominational.

So it was that, for example, traditional Rwandan music, musical instruments and tunes were not allowed in the church. The instruments were said to have been used for ancestral worship, while the musical tunes were too traditional, intimately connected to the customs and practices of the people – of foreign origin. Gradually, certain Rwandan instruments such as drums were accepted in song-leading, but not as a Rwandan expression of worship. Unfortunately, music is one avenue through which Rwandans express heartfelt love, joy, sorrow and praises. Rwandan music was, is and will continue to be our cultural expression of what is in our hearts, and such music is crucial to authentic Rwandan Christian worship. In the Rwandan culture, music supports and expresses values. Donald P. Hustad said it well: 'A unique musical expression gives identity to the entire culture; furthermore music is frequently used to accompany the society's most significant activities, and adds significance to those rituals. In this way music tends to reinforce the ideals of that society, whether they be political, social, or religious.'[1] To this day, there are still instruments that cannot be brought to church just because of the mindset left by the early missionaries, while Western tunes and instruments are still widely used.

Music and musical instruments were not the only things brought by missionaries; they also brought orders of service and styles of worship with them. One has to remember that in the colonial mission church era, African culture as a whole was viewed and treated as primitive, and in some cases even sinful. No wonder, then, that Rwandan culture was considered so inferior to the colonial missionaries' cultures and activities, with the result that the first converts supported the idea of sinfulness which was attributed to certain activities and objects and to certain values of the culture. Today, it would not be hard to convince people who have travelled around Africa that congregational singing of imported songs and tunes is not as powerful as people's praising God through melodies and styles of their own. I long to see churches in Rwanda singing in their own cultural expressions, reflecting the nativity of their melodies and rhythms by singing Rwandan tunes that will touch the Rwandan people's emotions and senses – and reflect their Christian commitment.

According to Ronald B. Allen and Gordon C. Borror, 'Music is one of the church's very best means of extolling God for who he is and what he has done, and one of the very best ways to spread the message of the gospel to unbelieving society.'[2] An unknown African sage once said, 'Melodies are one of the gifts we have from God. We ought to use them in the same manner as we use our bodies, hands, legs and thoughts. We express the nature of our thoughts by the way we speak. In the same way, we show our gratitude in praising God because of certain gifts by songs and hymns.'

Holy Communion elements, wedding ceremonies, dress styles, Christian names, the dos and don'ts of this and that in Christian community often reflect the desire in a missionary's heart to reproduce his home church. Church rules and standards may not be biblical, but a matter of what makes the missionaries feel comfortable. Both colonial and post-colonial missionaries were fine ambassadors of the Good News, and also of the cultural values they represented. I remember, for example, being told that I could not preach without wearing a tie. Some went as far as saying that to preach one should wear a suit with a tie, or at least a tie and a jacket over his shirt. Some pastors wore a tie and jacket over a worn-out shirt to satisfy this custom. While in Bible school, I remember students in preaching classes borrowing ties to wear while they preached.

My father was a very active man in the refugee camp where I grew up. After losing his job as a schoolteacher, he accepted God's call and a church's invitation to serve as a preacher. Each year that my father preached, he used to receive a complete suit and a tie at Christmas. Everyone in my family hated to see him in the oversized suits, and he always had to find someone to do up his tie for him. In his suit, my father looked like the incarnation of what K. P. Yohannan wrote: 'Conversion to Christ too often meant an informal adaptation of foreign cultural baggage and occidental prejudices as well.'[3]

In the early leadership years of President Mobutu of Zaire, Christian names and the wearing of Western clothing such as suits and ties were abolished. African names were to be used. (Amazingly, a great number of Zaireans have gone back to their Christian names and the wearing of Western suits, some as a means of revolt and sabotage of Mobutu's leadership.) Mobutu's early decision was appealing to his own country, and then to the younger population of many other African countries. As a high school student, I remember schoolmates who took on authentic African nicknames in imitation of what was going on in Zaire. The idea was to bring back and give Zairean cultural values the place they deserve among Zaireans, thus de-emphasizing – and perhaps degrading – European cultural practices and values. Immediately following his decision, Mobutu was seen by many missionaries as anti-Christian.

In Rwanda, as in many other African countries, certain customs and practices reflect colonial and denominational affiliation to both Europe and the West. To give some examples: Anglican and Episcopal church mission stations reflect the influence and cultural practices of the British missionaries; Free Methodists, Southern Baptists and Conservative Baptists reflect American influence; and the Catholic Church reflects more of a French and Belgian culture.

Christianity and education gave a new generation of young people the right to question the authority of non-Christians and the non-educated. As students going back home from boarding school, a friend of mine and I decided that since we were Christians we would stand against certain practices in the community, especially the drinking of alcohol and traditional dancing. Our decision brought us into conflict with not only our parents, but also elderly family friends. Our Christian teaching challenged the traditional beliefs of our parents, and we had no response or alternative solutions except to say that those practices were sinful. We were quick to provide them with the same answers we had received from our missionary teachers and that were culturally inappropriate and, in a sense, disrespectful.

Wherever the gospel has been proclaimed, of course, cultural values have been challenged. That is the nature of the gospel. The issue, however, is whether a Rwandan has to behave or adopt foreign cultural practices in order to become a Christian or to prove that he is one. Most cultural practices are an expression of people's beliefs, values and identity. There is no question that the Christian faith brought into Rwanda created internal conflict in the lives of church followers, who had to sort out how to behave in relation to both Christian teaching and traditional cultural expectations. A Rwandan does not have to abandon his culture to become Christian, but undoubtedly regeneration by the work of grace will bring changes in a Christian's individual life within his culture. This is more the work of the Holy Spirit than of missionaries, and is consistent with biblical teaching.

The missionaries worked in a culture that they believed needed to be civilized. Therefore, they had a mission not only to evangelize and bring people to Christian faith, but also to bring them out of their 'strange practices'. I remember a missionary friend saying that a Christian husband should not only help his wife with domestic duties, but also sit down and eat with his family as happens in the West. Now many educated men in Africa eat and share domestic duties with their wives even though it is not a common practice, and certainly not in Rwanda. Western practices have also dominated the culture surrounding marriage: traditional marriages have been challenged and are almost unacceptable to the Church. Polygamists have been denied roles in church and are sometimes made to feel unwelcome. Especially in cities, church practices, worship services and church rituals reflect more of the West than a true African identity.

The lifestyle of the early missionaries in the context of the colonial era did not differ very much from that of the colonialists. Missionaries were given free eggs, firewood and services as though they were any other colonialists, and they often emulated the practices of Western administrators, treating local people (Christians included) as uncivilized subordinates. The missionaries' relationship with local people may have been kinder, but was not necessarily one without a colonial attitude toward their church members. The love that was taught was not always practised.

In the early 1970s, I worked for missionaries to earn a little money for my Bible school training. The homes of missionaries on the compound where I worked had special cups in which they offered drinking water to employees on the compound, or to passing travellers. The specially designed cups were either margarine cans or biscuit tins, often hung on the back of outside kitchen doors, or near an outside storeroom. That way, when we asked for a drink, the missionaries or house boys could easily say, 'Pick up that tin and help yourself from the outside tap.' In so doing, they could avoid inviting us into their homes. As Bible school students and future church leaders, we perceived such 'hospitality' as an insult, and definitely a colonial mentality and attitude. As we drank water together we often used a Kirundi expression, '*Bgabundi ntigahera!*' meaning 'The attitude does not disappear!' Short-term missionaries were especially selective about whom they would let into their homes and sit in their chairs.

The barriers of colonialism have not been completely broken down; and where they have, new forms have risen.

The Christian mission made a significant contribution in Rwanda with both negative and positive impact on the lives of people. The gospel as presented by colonial-era missionaries would have been understood from a non-imperialistic perspective if missionaries had not been linked so much to social injustice, political involvement and the same lifestyle as that of the colonial administrators. Some of the missionaries' activities, ways of operating and relationships to the colonial administration appeared to be political: favouritism played out through discrimination in school systems; the taking of sides in political issues favouring one group of people over the other; and attitudes toward the nationals, the Rwandan culture and indigenous social structures. The practical lives of those proclaiming Christian principles and truths could not easily be reconciled with the Christian teachings of the gospel. The Catholic Christian mission's involvement in the affairs of the colonial administration and post-colonial governments somehow projected an indistinguishable state–church relationship. The discrepancies evidenced between Christian teachings and practices have left Rwandan people with questions to this day.

It is my conviction, especially in light of what happened in Rwanda recently, that when Christianity brings to another culture all the problems and questions of foreign cultural influences, it will remain foreign to the new land it hopes to reach with the gospel. If Christianity brings with it a strong challenge and determination to reconstruct the social and political aspects of the society but fails to address itself to the issues and needs of the new culture, it will not be heard, much less applied. As Bishop Nsengiyumva of the Catholic Church in Rwanda said, 'The Christian message is not being heard. After a century of evangelism we have to begin again because the best catechists, those who filled our churches on Sundays, were the first to go out with machetes in their hands.'4

I may sound too radical if I say that the Rwandan catechists and other church members involved in the 1994 genocide and mass killing may not have 'heard the message', but they still learned well from their early church planters and leaders. There is no one time in Rwandan church history when the Church was not involved in political games, ethnic divisions and discrimination, although yet on the outside, it appeared to be apolitical, continuing with the preaching of love, peace and justice; and Bishop Nsengiyumva's statement applies to all Christian missions in Rwanda. I know that receptivity plays a big role in gospel presentation and church planting in the missions. However, the early Catholic Church's concentration of energies on the Hutu elements of Rwandan society under the mission principle of receptivity – and the switching of emphasis when the Tutsis opened up to the gospel – presents an interesting field of study. The Church preached one thing and practised another. The same could be said of the Protestant Church side, save that the Protestants were in a sense a 'minority mission' without much voice, due to the relationship between the Catholic Church and the Belgian administration. Still, the Protestants spoke up regarding issues of discrimination and social injustice as it was observed in the behaviour of the Catholic Church and the colonial administration.

The early church involvement in colonial politics demonstrated the Western mentality that drew a sharp distinction between the two major groups of Rwandan society. The missionaries' lifestyle, the discrepancies between Christian teaching and practices, and the behaviour of certain Christian missions and missionaries that emulated the colonial administrators cost the Church its prophetic voice and weakened its position in the hearts of Rwandans.

FIVE

Dominance, Exploitation and the Seeds of Christianity

THE SEEDS OF Christianity in Rwanda were planted during difficult times of colonial dominance and exploitation. It was a time when the Rwandan traditional leadership and kingdom as a whole were facing an invasion which they had resisted successfully for a number of years, and it was a time when Arabs were active in slave trading of Africans in general to Europeans. Trading and colonial territorial expansion may have made it easy for missionaries to enter Rwanda, but their noble mission of the proclamation of good news may not have sounded much like good news to Rwandans.

The colonial era was one of European domination. Western nations in the business of colonialism were after power and opportunities for exploitation. Then, when successful, they were in the business of caring and helping people toward 'civilization' as they interpreted it. The colonialists did not initially and intentionally plan on developing people as a humanitarian act, but rather did what they did to achieve the intended outcomes.

Activities started by the colonialists cannot be dismissed as all bad; in fact, many wonderful things were done. But in the process dangerous mistakes and intentional exploitation of the people occurred. The colonial leadership restructured the indigenous leadership, and even the boundaries of the country. Before the colonists' arrival, kings had led the country according to their understanding and traditional beliefs. The colonial boundaries limited the country to colonial interests and problems of the time, the relationship and expansion plan of the powerful colonial masters having much to do with the tracing of boundaries. Belgium, Britain, France and Germany had much more say than the Rwandan kings, who were not even consulted at the time.

The domination and expansion of power and territory did not happen harmoniously. Wars were fought, lives lost and socioeconomic and political structures destroyed. The whole situation became unbearable to the natives of the land as they felt not only loss of power and control over their own affairs but also dehumanized. Such a feeling does great harm in societies where shame is emphasized, and in Rwanda saving face was very important. Kings, chiefs and other nobles were not used to being embarrassed in public: they were the 'macho-men' of the society, and more so the king, who was the final authority in the country next to God. The king's authority was uncontested, and to challenge his leadership meant death for the challenger, or war. So in a sense, the indirect rule strategy did help 'save face' for the traditional leaders, including the king. It probably also helped avoid what would have been face-to-face confrontations between the colonial administrators and the king with his chiefs – through the indirect rule policy the king and his chiefs ruled with more power and authority, based on the support of colonial administrators, especially under German rule. Much of the toughness shown by the indigenous Rwandan rulers, and which in some cases impressed the colonial rule, was in a sense a message to the Rwandan public to show that the Rwandan rulers had power. In reality, the power and authority belonged to the colonial officials, who made decisions behind the scenes: the king and his chiefs were but executors and implementers of the colonial policies.

Colonial power is discussed, and rightly so, as having been abusive and dehumanizing in nature. Rwandan nationals felt abused morally and physically as the colonials imposed hard labour for the purpose of exploiting the Rwandan people and land to enrich themselves. They physically abused and took advantage of the people, separating them from their families and their communities to attend to hard labour, whose only rewards seemed to be abusive insults, imposed taxes and slapping. Corporal punishment was the most difficult to bear for Rwandans, a male-oriented society where corporal punishment is meant for children and where among adults it was only used by abusive men against their wives. Again, the issue of shame: in this case, it made people learn ways of surviving under a colonial master who exercised such abuse through fellow Rwandans (in most cases a Tutsi chief or a leader of whatever project was under way). By this time, colonialists had developed a concept that the Tutsis were born leaders, a perspective encouraged by the early anthropologists and missiologists' belief that the Tutsis were partially of European extraction and therefore able to lead. This germinal idea – that Tutsis were inherently superior because of some European blood – became yeast to the ethnic tensions which were nurtured into the present fully blown hatred of each other.[1]

The Rwandan people, who went from one colonial master to another through wars that originated outside their influence and territory, had limited understanding of what was going on beyond their borders, but even less regarding the intent of the colonialists. The political manoeuvres, social behaviour and attitudes toward the Rwandans had manifested more and more a domineering and dehumanizing relationship that very soon taught the Rwandan people to learn to survive in all circumstances.

The timing of the missionaries' arrival in Rwanda was not in the best interest of the Christian mission and their preaching of the gospel; ironically it could have been. The missionaries broke new ground, made their own mistakes and had their opportunity to manifest their own beliefs and understanding of the people. They could have used the opportunity to distance themselves from the colonial attitudes and approach to Rwandan society. They could have expressed Christian love and therefore shown themselves to be different. But the early Christian missionaries often walked in the footsteps of their pioneers. The arrival of Bishop Joseph Hirth and his armed entourage, for example, sent a mixed message to the Rwandan traditional authorities about Hirth's missionary intent. Bishop Hirth was politely received by the Rwandan king's court because of the respect that the Rwandan traditional authorities had for the German colonial administrator, Herr Bethe. It is quite possible that the bishop would not otherwise have been received, due to the Rwandan rulers' fear of losing authority. Under other circumstances, the fact that the bishop was escorted by an armed group of men would have been another reason for rejection, or even violent confrontation.

To the Rwanda authorities, the pioneer Christian missionaries were viewed as either colonialists or agents of colonialism. In fact, they were considered by the traditional authorities to be the first real colonial settlers. The Catholic Christian missionaries in the country wanted land for settlement and for mission stations. They had come to stay and die in the country. They had come to evangelize and 'civilize' the nation. Their introduction to the king's court and demand of a mission plot at the same location must have been perceived by the king's court as an intrusion. Very suspicious of the armed missionary and his team, they sent them to a location away from the king's court where they were given land. The authorities did not expect Bishop Hirth and his team to last long in the location allocated to them for the simple reason that the area was the most problematic in the country. But the missionaries managed to stay long. In fact, they used the location as a base to expand their ministry field and influence in other places. The acquisition of land was an issue that contributed to a sense that colonial settlement was an inevitability. It also generated a belief that the king was losing control, and in a sense losing the country, to the colonial powers. The king's reference to one of the first White Fathers priest missionaries as 'the king of Hutus' was an indication and expression of how the traditional Tutsi administration felt about the missionaries. Later on, the Catholic mission experienced many instances of passive and violent resistance from both the population and the traditional authorities. The missionaries persisted, but their relationship with the Rwandan authorities did not improve.

Close collaboration of the White Fathers with the colonial powers misled the average person and sometimes the traditional authorities, and the missionaries' use of their relationships with the colonial administrators to accomplish goals and objectives previously denied by Rwandan traditional authorities clearly associated the missionaries with the colonial powers. To the traditional authorities, becoming a Christian meant disloyalty to cultural practices and traditional values, and in certain situations rebellion against traditional leadership. From the missionaries' perspective, victories against the devil's strongholds were being achieved, and then communicated back home through letters containing items of praises and lists of prayer requests. Material advantages, new economic structures, spiritual powers, even the generosity of missionaries in certain circumstances, were a threat and challenge to the traditional socioeconomic and political structures. Most of all, the traditional religion was being challenged, thus threatening certain beliefs and practices of the traditional leadership.

The change of colonial powers from German administration to the Belgian offers an interesting observation to be made concerning Christian mission. After the Germans lost Rwanda to the Belgians, the German Protestant mission that had been established in Rwanda left, and a Belgian Protestant mission took over. Regardless of the fact that this transfer may have gone well with the two missions involved, and that the transfer probably was a strategic move to be in line with the administration that was taking over, one can't help but look at the situation analytically with regard to the context. First of all, the Rwandan traditional authority had enjoyed largely positive relationships with the German administration. The Catholic Christian mission had sought to challenge the country's socioeconomic and political structure in disfavour of the traditional authorities and indeed had raised issues toward that end. Still, the German administration clearly stayed away from any change suggested by the Church, and operated through existing structures with little interference to the tradi-

tional leaders. Often the Catholic missionaries had listened to the complaints of their new converts and made moves to protect them by appealing
to colonial authorities rather than traditional. The German Protestant
mission, by contrast, was relatively quiet, and stayed within the policies and
political orientation of the colonial administration, with no involvement in
the politics of the country. One could say that while they were there to
support and represent interests of their country while bringing the gospel
to the subjects of their empire, the Catholics' desire was still with a Christian kingdom in mind and the subsequent desire for a change of the socioeconomic and political structure.

The German administration had often proved to be supportive of the
traditional Rwandan authority, and the German Protestant mission
followed suit. When the new Belgian administration arrived, however, a
new Protestant mission from Belgium took over from the German Protestants. Suddenly the Catholic mission, with strong convictions against the
traditional authority, rose to be a 'power player' in the Belgian colonial
administration of Rwanda. Strong relationships and collaboration between
the mission and the colonial administration developed and, to a certain
extent, they became indistinguishable in political affairs. The entrusting of
schools and other social services to the Catholic mission, funded by the
Belgian colonial administration, elevated the mission from a mere evangelistic and church planting outreach to a key political entity in Rwanda. This
deep involvement with the Belgian colonial administration, and the roles
given people like Bishop Classe, have to this day made it impossible for the
Catholic mission to escape from being associated with the injustice, colonial
acts of exploitation, and manipulation of conflicts between the two major
groups (Hutu and Tutsi) of the Banyarwanda (Hutu, Tutsi and Twa).

Local Rwandan leaders were suspicious of the missionaries' role in the
colonial structure. Many Rwandans did not believe the intent of their
ministry was what it was explained to be. Simply put, the colonial officials'
image did not help that of the first missionaries in the country. The fact that
local politicians and the non-converted community of the time kept the
first Catholic missionaries at arm's length is a good indication of the missionaries' image as perceived by the king and his nobles. The missionaries
were always viewed in conjunction with the colonial masters' intent.
Masters and missionaries were all perceived as being white Europeans who
served each other in a sinister form of Western imperialism. You often hear
people saying that colonialists came conquering territories, while their
fellow countrymen pacified the population in the name of Christianity.

What the missionary community had that the colonial masters did not have, however, was a calling to Christian ministry and a Christian world-view to guide their relationships with people. Unfortunately, the 'Christian worldview' held by most colonial missionaries was very much shaped by their native culture and colonial policy. They did not necessarily view the Rwandan within the full biblical framework of all human beings having been created equal before God, and with equal potential of becoming what God intended them to be.

Missionaries took advantage of the colonial system not only to advance their cause, but also personally to benefit from its policies and practices. Colonial policies contributed to the missiological theology and foundation of the Christian mission in Rwanda, and the Christian missions played an essential role in the domination and administration of colonial rule under both the Germans and Belgians. The missionaries spread European influence in all corners of the country, provided major social services on behalf of the colonial administration and contributed to the leadership and political development of the country. To this day, whenever social injustice and condescending attitudes are attributed to the 'colonial masters', Christian missionaries are often included in that group.

The Rwandan people initially observed the relationships that existed between the Catholic missionaries, the Protestants and the colonial administrators, and they quickly adopted a compromising, accommodating model of cooperation that they observed working in colonial relationships. From 1916 to the 1950s they learned how to gain power and wield influence from the close relationships and collaboration that existed between the Catholic missionaries and Belgian colonial officials. The relationships of both the Protestant and the Catholic churches to the two governments that spanned the 1960s through the 1994 genocide acts were nothing new, but an imitation and faithful implementation of the learned and modelled lessons of the colonial era. The indirect divide-and-rule approach and subsequent exclusion of one ethnic group from social services, public office and educational institutions was also adopted (though not in full) by the government and Christian missions alike. The policy of *Iringaniza* (total exclusion of one ethnic group) in most cases was not different from the colonial discriminatory school system executed at the expense of Rwandan children of the time. And the silence of many Christian missions in the face of such injustices was deafening.

The divide-and-rule political approach is also observed in Christian mission work. I call it 'divide-and-minister'. Unfortunately, such practices have no biblical grounds and therefore are not fitting in Christian leadership and Christian church. The original 'divide-and-minister' approach to church planting in Rwanda started when Bishop Joseph Hirth was refused his request to build a mission station at the king's court. As discussed earlier, Hirth was instead given land in another location, where he settled and found the Hutus to be quite receptive and open to the gospel. The resistance of the Rwandan king, who was trying to hold on to the traditional religion based on a cult of sacred warrior-kingship, gave a powerful legitimacy to the monarchy. The nobles and their subjects were loyal followers of their king and therefore did not convert. The early conclusion of the missionaries was to be that Tutsis were impossible to convert. The missionaries' emphasis and work among the Hutus was not necessarily based on studied conclusions of gospel 'resistance and receptivity', but rather quick conclusions based on a colonial mentality. This is why critics of what the country has experienced over the years portray early evangelism as the most subtle and dangerous incursion of Western imperialism on the local society.

This is not simply a Catholic issue; rather, it is an issue of the colonial outlook of early missionaries – Catholic and Protestant alike – who encountered any culture that was different from their own. It happens that in Rwanda, the deep politicization of the Church originates from the Catholic mission leaders switching Christian church allegiance, evangelism and leadership emphasis, from Hutu to Tutsi and back to the Hutus. Politicians might belong now here and now there to confuse people and seek political support. But for a Christian mission to play political games that stand and support one ethnic group today and another tomorrow is not a Christian testimony; instead it shows a lack of Christian principles and guiding biblical theology.

The seeds of Christianity were sown in the weeds of colonial dominance and the exploitation of human beings. The weeds did not allow for a strong Christian rooting and subsequent spiritual development among Rwandans. Different evangelistic approaches and a concerted strategy of Christian discipleship is needed to address the issues that contributed to the destruction of Christian testimony and witness in Rwanda. The Christian missions evangelized Rwandan people, established schools and hospitals, and developed social services. But, with individual exceptions, they generally failed to model a true Christian life. There is a profound need for godly men and women to teach biblical Christian living in countries like Rwanda – and throughout the world, because where it is not Tutsi and

Hutu, it is white and black, Hispanic and Anglo-American, Serb and Croat, Irish and English. People like to draw lines based on ethnic identity, colour of skin and geographical locations. The truth of the matter is that the heart and origin of such line-drawing is the sinful nature of humankind. Even if all people were of the same ethnic background and the same nationality, there would still be found ways to draw lines – by those within and without the Church who have not yet understood their identity in Christ.

SIX

The Death of a
Credible Christian Testimony

CHRISTIAN MISSIONS AND Rwandan politics were intertwined from the early stages of the introduction of Christianity in Rwanda. As outlined in previous pages, the Catholic mission's strategy was to reach first the traditional leaders. According to the instruction given to them by Cardinal Lavigerie, the Catholic missionary movement's founder, converting the traditional local leaders would be likely to produce mass conversions, but the reality of the Rwandan infrastructure forced the missionaries to find an alternative to this heartfelt strategy. This led to what is known today in mission circles as 'the homogeneous principle', which in essence means focusing the work of preaching the gospel on one defined group at a time. In Rwanda, its early expression was a Hutu peasant church, because for several years at the outset of Rwandan missions, the Catholic Church opted to work almost exclusively with Hutu peasant society.

The initial refusal of local leaders, the king, chiefs and other nobles to cooperate with the original church planting strategy contributed to the Catholic missionaries' battle against the native sociopolitical structure. Had the Rwandan king and his chiefs agreed to the proposal brought by the missionaries, the priests would have taken a different approach. The paradoxical behaviour, attitudes and approach of the Catholic Church were evident as they first created division through condemning a socioeconomic practice (*ubuhake*) as ethnic discrimination, then switching allegiance from the Hutus to the Tutsis and back to the Hutus over the next few decades. Their unpredictable approach and political game-playing called into question their testimony, missionary vision and prophetic role.

The early Catholic mission did not agree with the German colonial political philosophy and policy and did not support the Germans' indirect rule approach, as they felt that it supported social oppression and unjust practices by the Tutsis over the Hutu peasants. The missionaries' evangelistic message to the oppressed and the poor emphasized a determination to end 'the oppressive sociopolitical structure' as they viewed it, and they offered protection to early converts. This stance brought them to an early conflict with the German colonial administrators and the Rwandan traditional leaders, but the missionaries were successful at reaching the Hutu peasant community. Their message, economic and material offers, protection and political approach were appealing to the peasant Hutu community, while the Tutsi leadership resisted them. The Hutus had nothing to lose and much to gain by converting to the new religion, while the Tutsis (especially the king, chiefs and others in the middle class) had much at risk. The same has proved to be true in most privileged classes of different societies.

The Protestant missionaries who worked during the German colonial administration in Rwanda were by contrast on good terms with the administration, supporting the colonial indirect leadership approach and leaving the colonial officials alone. It did not take long before the pre-dominantly Catholic attitudes and 'conclusive' beliefs that had labelled the Tutsis 'anti-Christian' and 'unconvertible' were proved wrong in the 1930s by the conversion of the Tutsi king, certain nobles and chiefs and, further, by the 1936 revival.

This mistaken attitude towards Tutsis was illustrated by a missionary friend of mine. Frustrated with young Tutsis' questions regarding Christian salvation, he responded angrily to the young men saying, 'That is my problem with Tutsis. They try to rationalize what is received by faith.' Not to offend him, I gently smiled and politely said, 'They want to test your apologetics.' Indeed, the problem is not rationalization; the problem was that missionaries did not expect questions of understanding from the nationals, but expected them to just believe what they were told without questioning.

The Catholic Church's involvement in Rwandan political affairs, through the development of close relationships and associations with the Belgian colonial administration, contributed to what most Rwandan people viewed as a double standard in Christian mission behaviour. The early German colonial relationship with the Protestant Christian mission had angered the French-based Catholics, who saw the Protestants as more favoured because of their German background. Their unfavourable relationship resulted in the Catholic mission's anti-German colonial approach, bringing the two to a sharp disagreement, and this conflict became apparent to the Rwandan population, especially in political circles. When the Rwandan king tried to take advantage of the conflict, it raised tensions between the king and the White Fathers, so the Catholic mission opted quietly and continuously to work with grassroots Rwandans, determined eventually to bring about social change. While church leaders might have viewed Rwandan society as uneducated and perhaps unaware of the political role the missionaries were seeking, the nationals actually were observant and therefore learning from their most admired Christian mission leaders. It was not surprising, then, that a larger number of the Rwandan population's 86 per cent believed to be Christian participated in the 1994 genocide of Tutsis and mass killing of Hutu moderates. Remembering the Kinyarwanda saying, '*Wibuba uhetse ukabawigisha uwo mu umugongo*', meaning if you steal when carrying a youngster on your back you are teaching the youngster to steal, could this be what happened as a result of Catholic involvement in power politics while they were simultaneously preaching good news and its message of unity, love and peace? This is where most Rwandans, at least the victims of the 1950s Belgian political move, which enjoyed the consent and support of the Catholic Church, question the sincerity and Christian testimony of the colonial mission.

The Belgian takeover from the German government quickly brought the Catholic missionaries 'out of hiding' to a more open and vocal advocacy of sociopolitical change in the country. The Catholic mission's experience in Rwandan society and grassroots sociopolitical structure gave them an advantage over the Belgian colonials, and because Belgium was largely a Catholic nation, there was an inherent Catholic influence throughout the Belgian administration and politics. The Minister of Colonies was himself a devout Catholic with strong ties to the church leadership in Belgium. The Catholic missionaries not only gained favour in the eyes of their fellow countrymen, but also took on a new role in the colonial administration, serving as advisors and providing the administration with the orientation they badly needed. In the process, the Catholic mission was able to advance its views of the sociopolitical structure and openly worked for change, also making it hard for Protestant missions to advance their work.

In the 1950s the Hutu priests who had seen and observed the White Fathers' political manoeuvres accused their European counterparts of indifference to what they had initially called social injustice, and brought out the Europeans' failure to push political leaders for reform. Knowing the White Fathers' historical complaints about what they had perceived and labelled as 'social injustice', and knowing that in the process of political manoeuvring, the Fathers had moved from being leaders of a Hutu-dominated church to leading a Tutsi-dominated élite church, the Hutus who had been educated in the Catholic schools – especially the seminaries – formed a counter-élite. As both the political and the church structures continued to develop, the Catholic Church influenced the Belgian administration to switch their allegiance away from Tutsis to Hutus, making it possible for the Hutus to seize power in 1959–60.

The Protestant Christian missions were largely apolitical in their approach to the Rwandan sociopolitical structure. The first Protestant missionaries to enter the country supported the indirect German colonial approach and in so doing, raised no sociopolitical issues. A small minority in the country, they were not highly visible and had limited personal influence; their interest was in evangelism, leaving the social issues alone. The victory of the Belgians over the Germans made the Protestant Church that was favoured by the German administrators leave the country. The next Protestants present in Rwanda (arriving after much Catholic resistance) were the Seventh Day Adventists, and shortly after them the Church Missionary Society (CMS) with origins in England. The CMS came via Uganda and, being out of favour with the Belgian colonial officials and the Catholic Church, developed a relationship with the Rwandan king within weeks of their arrival. Dissatisfied with the relationships and behaviour of both the Catholic missionaries and Belgian colonial administrators, the king sought ways of balancing the Catholics' influence by giving special attention to the British missionaries. The move did not appeal politically and diplomatically to the Belgian colonial officials and White Fathers, but made matters worse: the Catholics were afraid to lose the country to Protestantism, and the Belgians were concerned about CMS's British influence. The CMS apolitical stance, focus on the gospel and hard work won praise from the king – if the CMS missionaries had political convictions as to how Rwandan society should look, they suspended them for the sake of a Christian witness and the unity of the community around them.

But the time came when Protestant (and especially the Anglican British) missionaries decided to take strong stands on social and political issues, motivated by the identity card based on ethnicity. The prayer life, Christian testimony and witness of both nationals and missionaries of CMS background led to the 1936 revival that swept East Africa. It is probably no coincidence that the identity card was introduced in 1936 by the Belgian administration with the support of the Catholic mission. (It passed into use despite CMS's uncompromising expression of what they believed.) The issuing of identity cards was followed by the introduction of forced hard labour that separated men from their families and community: taking people to the Belgian Congo's mining and timber industries, it brought starvation to Rwanda. The CMS is said to have addressed the problem and given their views against the identification card based on ethnic distinction. For years the Anglicans were viewed as being more pro-Tutsi than other Protestant missions, even though the Protestant missions chose an apolitical public orientation until the 1960s.

The presence overwhelmingly identified in Rwanda as 'Christian' was that of the Catholic missions. Its history might not characterize it as always living to be light and salt: its strategy seemed to be based upon looking at Rwandans as anything but a nation, and what began as a typical 'change agent' approach in missions developed into pitting Hutus against Tutsis. It was too convenient in the eyes of many Rwandans that the Catholics switched their allegiance from Hutus to Tutsis after Tutsis began to convert. All along, the Catholic mission worked to influence and where possible control political machinations, even through involvement in the formation of political parties. The switch of Catholic allegiance from Tutsis back to educated Hutus fed the perception that the Church not only approved but also participated in the 1959 revolution and mass killing of Tutsis. There was hardly to be found a characterization of the Church as preachers of the good news or advocates of love, peace and unity, much less as people who believed in being created equal and in God's image.

There were times during the German administration when the White Fathers were asked to keep out of political matters. Rather, they became a Christian mission that got involved in drawing lines and contributing to the building of invisible walls, pitting Hutus against Tutsis throughout their history in Rwanda. As I look back in the context of what has happened recently, it is clear that involvement like Bishop Classe's attempt to bring down the Rwandan king in the 1920s affected the Church's testimony. Through his influence, Classe convinced Belgian administrators to depose the king – Classe did not himself take action, but the then-Belgian governor did. The Catholic missionaries' prophetic role changed after the mass conversion of both Hutus and the Tutsi rulers. Given their success across the social strata, the Catholic Church believed it had the right to influence sociopolitical issues, even regarding leadership and the formation of a government of choice, and this attitude put the Church ministry at risk, as we will see later. The Church, outspoken as it was, could not effectively minister to people. To this day I believe that for the sake of the unity of believers, direct and vocal political involvement should be avoided. Emphasis should rather be given to practical Christian living that models change. The Catholic Church should have encouraged Christians to live a moral life, demonstrating the qualities of salt and light.

The Catholic Church was fully involved in the Hutu Manifesto, most Hutus behind the movement being a Catholic-trained élite who had learned very well from people such as Bishop Classe and his fellow priests. The key issue was the Tutsi political monopoly, an issue that became irrelevant when the Catholic Church switched allegiance from the Hutus to the Tutsis immediately following the mass conversion of Tutsi chiefs, nobles and their followers. Hutus were silently ignored until the late 1950s, when Catholic missionaries declared their support of the Hutu movement born in 1957. Tutsis reacted to the Hutu movement by forming UNAR (Union Nationale Rwandaise), a movement critical of both the Church and the Belgian residents for their actions that had divided the country. The result of both Church and colonial politicking against the Tutsi leadership was characterized by political turmoil and upheavals against Tutsis and was, in a sense, the start of the genocide which saw its climax in 1994. Many Tutsis found refuge in parishes, others were protected by church mission station staff and especially European priests. Still, there were reports among Rwandans of certain church leaders' roles in the killings by pointing fingers at victims. I have not heard of priests who killed, but it is painfully clear that many of them observed the killing and said nothing. Others encouraged killing of Tutsis through what they said, or actions they took. The majority of Catholic missionaries wanted a Hutu Catholic-educated leadership. Political parties formed were closely linked to religious beliefs and faith.

Some will argue that, in the 1950s, the Catholic Church leaned toward Hutus while Anglican Protestants were pro-Tutsi. In any event, the 1994 genocide derives from deep historical divisions nurtured in the Church. Although people like Bishop Perraudin struggled to restore church testimony shortly before that holocaust, it was too late. Before him, other White Father priests had been militant advocates of political reform. A Christian magazine founded in the early 1930s to propagate the faith became a communication channel for politics by the late 1940s. There were divisions in the Catholic Church among Catholic Tutsis and Hutus. Whatever was going on, the Catholic Church failed to address the divisions inside the Church and therefore could not offer a solution to the masses. Nor would they bring about a harmonious understanding among the élite Hutu and Tutsi within their ranks. New missionaries viewed the 'pioneers' as slow in bringing about reforms. Young and fresh out of Europe, they felt they could effect change quickly and they immediately embarked on the road of reforms. At some point Christian testimony was forgotten and political ideologies put before the church agenda.

Across Africa, the formation of the *évolués*, or groups of intellectuals, in the 1950s moved people more towards independence and this drove colonialists and the Church into the final stages of their divide-and-rule leadership approach. The seed of division that was planted much earlier did not allow the *évolués* from both Hutus and Tutsis to work together; instead, they remained divided along ethnic group lines. Somewhere in the process, the Church lost its prophetic role. It could have been an instrument of positive change as a witnessing, worshipping and serving community – by acting as salt and light. But the Church in Rwanda failed to give warning, or even advice, concerning the actions of its own people, while playing political power games. The Church failed to defend the rights of all, whether the attack came through abuse of power or through dehumanizing propaganda.

For the Catholic Church, the departure of king Musinga in 1931 was a remarkable victory. As a native Rwandan, however, I believe the church leaders' whole involvement in the business of political reforms, intended to change traditional structure and establish a government of choice, was not the calling of the Church. As a Christian, I feel that the Catholic church leaders were not aware of Romans 13. Submission to governing authorities was of no consideration. But since the authority of the king did not go along with either the missionaries' or the colonial administrators' political orientations, the king was to be deposed and another elected at their consent. The rebellion against the Rwandan king's authority was unbiblical: to settle Rwandan political matters, it probably would have been better to pay attention to what was being done wrong by both the White Fathers and the colonial administrators themselves.

The Hamitic thesis generalized by Catholic missiologists, according to which Tutsis are from a Caucasian race,[1] divided (and continues to divide) the Rwandan community. Tutsis were viewed and still are referred to as 'born leaders'; one European writer went as far as saying that the Tutsis were of a tanned skin before becoming black.[2] Their stature brought them close to that of Europeans, who therefore could easily work with them. The Hamitic origin was appealed to in the 1959 Hutu Manifesto, stressing division and echoing what was taught by Catholic missionaries on the subject, and Bishop Perraudin came out loud and clear in support of the Hutu Manifesto. The Belgian government supported the Hutus during the 1959 killing of Tutsis; it did not discourage the Church from political involvement, but sought its continued support instead.

The cost of politics has been a further deterioration of Christian testimony.

Part Three

—

The Credibility Crisis

SEVEN

As If Nothing Happened

FOR SOME, THE programme of Tutsi extermination was a dream come true. It is not only a 1994 phenomenon; the actual plan and desire to exterminate Tutsi started in 1950, and although the triggering factors were many, they could be classified under two headings: colonial dominance and Hutu revolt. In 1959 the war against the Tutsi left many dead; others, including my family, managed to run for their lives.

The Belgians had no desire to relinquish power, planning to hold on in Rwanda as long as they could; but change was happening all around Africa. Nationalistic movements were in full swing across Africa, and some had the ear of the Western world. Today's well-known pioneers and heroes of independent movements were at work, and Rwandans were fully aware of what was happening in other parts of their world. Neither Belgian colonial officials in Rwanda nor the Belgian government itself were sure of what might happen in a country with a centralized traditional leadership and the influence of a Rwandan king among his people. One thing is certain: both the Belgian colonial administrators and the Catholic Church never trusted the Rwandan traditional leadership, and they had already seen and tested the potential of the Rwandan king and his entourage. The early resistance of the Rwandan leaders to European influence was still fresh in the minds of the White Fathers, and as organized as the Rwandan kingdom was, there was reason for the colonials to be afraid. The Catholic Christian mission had desired change that would favour Hutus virtually from the days of their arrival in Rwanda, and they were still looking for the day this might happen. As we have seen, the switch of allegiance from Hutu to Tutsi was not a natural change of church growth strategy, but a political move on the part of the Catholic Christian mission. The change brought them to where they had hoped to begin: working with leaders to influence their subjects in Christian matters. Toward this goal, the Catholic Church succeeded with both the traditional leadership and the colonial power. Both the Belgian government and the Catholic Church wanted to maintain dominance in the tiny, beautiful 'country of a thousand hills', but this was not about to happen naturally: the natives of the land also wanted to lead themselves and bring their country to independence. The signals of the Rwandans' intentions were clear, and the two powers of European origin were quick at reading them, and hastened to find a solution in their favour. The most appealing was that of the White Fathers' early desire to see the Hutus in power and leadership of the country. The two European powers in Rwanda knew very well that if the Tutsi were in power with full authority, they would not be able to push their European agendas. Rather, they would have to 'dance' according to the local Rwandan leadership's tune. The Rwandan Tutsi leaders were intelligent and confident of their leadership capability. Therefore, they were most likely to follow their own agenda. The early White Fathers and other colonial officials viewed Hutus' leadership as mediocre. To the majority of Europeans in Rwanda at that time, Hutus were viewed as 'cute little followers' and excellent farmers, while the Tutsis were said to be born leaders.

During the 1994 genocide, we invited a missionary couple to our house for dinner. While still at table, the husband asked what I thought was going to happen in Rwanda. This was purely a question of prediction. The killing was still going on, the RPF was fighting to stop the genocide, and all the while a number of Hutus were steadily marching across the borders of Zaire and Tanzania. I said to him that I believed the RPF was going to capture the country, and that they were going to establish a broad-based government. His response to my answer surprised me. First he did not believe the RPF could capture the country, and in his opinion if they did, that was the end of Hutus and his work in Rwanda. When I asked why, he said that he feared for his life due to his relationship with the Hutus. Then he added that the Tutsis were 'too clever and intelligent' to work with. When I pushed him a little bit more, better to understand what he meant about the Tutsis' cleverness and intelligence, he backed off and simply said, 'With Tutsi leadership, the Hutus will be back on their knees in no time. Tutsis should never be allowed back in Rwanda. Besides,' he argued, 'we don't have a Tutsi who can lead our church. What are we supposed to do?' I jokingly offered to be their church leader, but at the same time asked him a question as to why they had to have a Tutsi. His answer was that it had always been a practice in Rwanda to find a church leader with political connections and easy contacts to facilitate church business. He tried to quote me the 'It's not what you know, it's who you know' principle which, incidentally, I have found to be a universal principle rather than a unique characteristic of Rwanda or Africa as some may be led to believe.

The Hutus started their movement within the Catholic Church and were given full attention and publicity in the Catholic publications. Catholic priests, working with the Hutu élite, managed to get the Hutu into Belgium to rally the support of politicians who were aware of what was going on in Rwanda. The results of the visit to Belgium were fruitful for the Hutu effort.

Toward the end of 1959, Rwanda was experiencing the political manoeuvres and upheavals of what was an obvious power struggle between the Hutus and Tutsis. Behind the power struggle were the Catholic missionaries and the colonial officials, fuelling the conflict in favour of their future in the country. In fact, Tutsi leaders of the time strongly believe that certain leaders of the Catholic Church and colonial administration were fully involved in the planning of the political revolt that resulted in a move toward ethnic extermination of Tutsis and that climaxed in 1994. In that genocide of the Tutsis and mass killing of Hutu political moderates, Hutu politicians were quoted as saying, 'The 1959 mistake should not be repeated.' The 'mistake' of 1959 was that of not having eliminated the Tutsis entirely. In 1994, they were prepared long before the actual genocide started to exterminate the Tutsi. The word used by Hutu extremists was '*Gutsembatsemba*', literally translated 'wipe out' or 'exterminate'. That is what they tried to do, but as the Rwandan people themselves say, '*Umwanzi agucira icyobo, Imana ikagucira icyanzu*' ('An enemy may dig you a trap hole, but God will make an escape way').

The outcome of the 1959 conflict might not have been exactly what the colonial administration and the Catholic Church leadership desired. They were both too deeply involved to withdraw easily, so they called upon the Belgian government to help control the situation. The Belgian soldiers sent to Rwanda made matters worse for the Tutsis by fighting for the Hutus, and the result was that the Hutus gained control. That much was a goal accomplished. But the fallout included thousands of Tutsi killed, and others exiled by the hundreds of thousands. Houses were burned and looted, and Tutsi property confiscated. Unfortunately, the media technology was not what it is today, and little coverage (if any) was given to this event through radio, telegrams and newspapers in countries with interests in Rwanda.

Immediately following the 1959 carnage, thousands were suffering in refugee camps in the neighbouring countries. The signs of war and the mass killing of Tutsis were everywhere. But it was business as usual in Rwanda; life continued as though nothing had happened. Churches resumed their activities with little or no remorse about the violence. Stories often told among Tutsi refugees were that the Catholic priests had resumed preaching messages of love and peace. A Catholic priest who was a friend of my father wanted him back in the country and crossed the Burundi border into the temporary refugee camp where we stayed to talk. He promised that he would be able to protect our family and secure our looted goods and property, and regretted that Christians had been involved in the looting and burning of homes. He also indicated that if my father had been at home on the night of the attack, he would have been killed. My father had been on the list of the 'most wanted' in the area where we lived. When my father asked about Hutus he knew with a desire to know about their welfare, the priest indicated that they were back into their activities as usual but acknowledged that there were unusual movements among the seemingly educated individuals in our former home district.

During the first year of the Tutsis' life in exile as refugees, church leaders (more so those of the Catholic Church) reached out to their friends or relatives and tried to get them back into the country. The Catholic mission leaders and certain national church leaders could ensure protection of whomever they wanted to return to Rwanda, or provide an exit to join family or relatives in exile. Separated families worked through the missions to trace their loved ones and to be reunited where possible. The Catholic Church in Rwanda had a powerful base of power due to its role in the revolution, and was in a position to influence change of any kind. Unfortunately, it does not seem that the Church wanted the Tutsis back, and if it did, there were no clear steps taken by the church leadership to address the refugee problem, or even condemn the evil acts that led to thousands of deaths and sent hundreds of thousands into exile. Was the Church in Rwanda in a position to plead for the return of the Rwandan refugees in exile? Given its status at that time, and the role it played in the bloody massacres, I believe it could have contributed significantly. Even if there had been no government response, if the Church had done its part, the international community would probably have echoed the message. But the Church's silence contributed to the perception of its previous political involvement, thus indicating its support of ethnic distinction and separation. And if the Catholic Church's militant spirit regarding social issues during the German colonial rule and politics of the 1950s was a sincere response to social injustice and oppression, surely the Church would have spoken up for the gross human rights abuses of the period from the 1960s to 1994. What do we say of the Rwandan church's theology regarding God's creation of humankind? Is this an issue for Hutu and Tutsi alone, or an issue that Christians around the world need to address?

Word-of-mouth reports coming into refugee camps said that of church attenders who confessed to having killed Tutsis, either to Hutu or to some European priests, some were told that God had given them up for death, while others were sent home with the words, 'Go my son, killing a Tutsi is not sin' ('*Kwica umututsi si icyaha*'). Unlike the 1994 genocide, church mission stations were safe ground for many Tutsis following the 1959 attacks. Tutsis who survived and decided to remain in Rwanda were integrated in the Church, but were always reminded of who they were and their status in the community. Even though the Church tended to be sympathetic to the social status and conditions of the surviving Tutsis in general, both the Catholic and Protestant churches (and more so the leadership) were politicized enough to keep in line with what the Rwandan government wanted. It did not matter about belief, the biblical teaching of love and unity, or one's view of humankind; the Church chose to listen and move with the political agenda of the country.

In 1963 a fresh rash of killing, similar to that of 1959, resumed, and the Church remained silent. Tutsis involved in church ministries and faithful church attenders were intimidated, and a few were killed, though not directly in the church or by the Church. But the Church's silence allowed some of the church leaders actually to take advantage of the situation to reshuffle their church staff. It was a prime opportunity to remove Tutsis and replace them with Hutus, while Tutsis not removed from their positions were often given church posts no one wanted. Although the 1963 killings targeted Tutsis and left hundreds dead, a few managed to run for their lives to exile, while those with no way out remained and learned ways to survive through compromises that were dehumanizing in nature. The whole of Rwanda – Church, social structure, economic and political systems alike – was anti-Tutsi. The anti-Tutsi spirit and policy was tough, and practised in all sectors of the sociopolitical life of the country under the policy of '*equilibre*', observed in the Church as well. Life was continually frustrating for Tutsis throughout the first Rwandan presidential regime. For survival, many Tutsis changed their identification cards to reflect a different ethnic name. This way, their children could be educated and then secure jobs after their schooling. Where people were not eliminated or exterminated physically, plans to were made to exterminate them from academic and professional development. The result would systematically ensure exclusive Hutu intellectual development and homogeneous involvement in all aspects of the affairs of the country.

In 1973, killings targeted schools in certain parts of the country that had a large population of Tutsis who had survived the killings of 1959 and 1963. The Christian environment itself, and more so Catholic institutions, seem to have been the main targets of the 1973 massacres. During these events, Christians of all denominations seemed completely to ignore Christian teachings. While they abandoned their fellow church members, Church leaders forgot their flocks and saw things through Tutsi or Hutu lenses rather than from a Christian perspective. Many Christians believers decided to cease relations with their Tutsi Christian friends out of fear of the consequences; but a few courageous believers risked their lives, sacrificed their status and stood with the 'unwanted and death-deserving' Tutsis. A friend of mine, now in Rwanda, wrote to his friend overseas, 'I will never forget. I will never forget that young girl who, hearing a military car approaching our house in Kigeme, took my hand strongly and pulled me out into a plantation of sorghum, in which the trees were high enough to hide. We knew that our lives were in the hands of the Lord.'

Politicization was renewed in the 1970s. Rwandan people in exile had hoped that the second Rwandan government under then-president Habyarimana would call for repatriation of the Rwandan refugees. The early months of Habyarimana leadership offered some hope, but it did not take long before he actually strengthened the Hutu dominance and requested Rwandan refugee host countries to offer the refugees naturalization or permanent residency. The Rwandan government's rationale for the naturalization request was based on the Habyarimana's egoistic view of the size of the country. He clearly stated that the country was too small, and that therefore Rwandan refugees should stay in their host countries. The statement was, of course, unwelcome and in fact detrimental to the Rwandan refugee community. It fuelled their determination to regain their home.

The new government established a politicization agenda, and the colonial master committed to rebuilding the country without the thousands of Rwandan refugees in exile. The Catholic Christian mission leadership was given a permanent role in the new government. The new Rwandan president and most of his top leadership were students of the Catholic theologians who taught social justice; they were a Hutu élite who had founded a political party, which was supported by church leadership and the colonial administration, and which was based on ethnic lines. Church support for a political position such as that held by the two previous Rwandan governments is no different from that of church agencies or even governments that have supported apartheid on the basis of racial discrimination. The Catholic Church accepted to serve on the central committee of both Rwandan presidential governments. The Church sold its testimony from the day that it supported an identity card based on ethnic differentiation, and became heavily involved in political agendas of both the colonial and traditional leadership to secure a platform for speaking out on social issues such as those of oppression. It actively, and successfully, pursued the deposition of the Rwandan king Musinga to replace him with his son; it stayed politically involved and manoeuvred through governments for its own ends.

After the killings of the late 1950s and the formation of the new government, there was no sign of repentance from church leadership, or a visible desire from them to call church members that were involved in the killing to repentance or reconciliation. The sinful acts the church leadership and adherents did against Christian brothers, sisters and the Rwandan Tutsi population went unnoticed. Certain individuals are known to have taken steps that led them to reach out to survivors and even to return looted and confiscated properties; but these were sporadic individual acts that did not gain public notice; and since they did not, they could not speak to the hurting Rwandan refugee.

In the initial refugee days of the 1959 killings, Rwandan refugees in the neighbouring countries suffered; and because of their suffering, some were willing to go back to their country regardless of the result. The Rwandan government (and some parishes) were publicly promoting peace and calling for return of the refugees, but church leaders aware of the government's plan advised individual refugees to stay away until peace had really returned and the government was serious about their promises. Those who returned toward the end of 1959 ran away again in 1960, as was my own experience in the care of my parents.

The Rwandan refugee community in the neighbouring countries endured difficulties and survived through seemingly hopeless situations. Some had lost hope of ever returning to their homeland after the failure of the 1960s attacks by refugee guerrilla groups known as 'Inyenzi'. But then came the birth and rising of the RPF (Rwandan Patriotic Front) movement. The RPF inspired people and gave hope to the hopeless Rwandans scattered in different parts of the world, especially to those who were in hostile host countries. By this time, what started as refugee camps were more like refugee settlements. Christian mission agencies with an interest in reaching out to Rwandan refugee communities in host countries started evangelistic ministries and planted churches that were later turned over to the national churches of the host countries. Burundi national leaders worked among Rwandan communities, but often gave special attention to their own people, while ignoring the needs of the Rwandan refugee people. Sometimes Burundi churchmen lacked resources; at other times their response to Rwandan refugees was based on church and secular politics. The Rwandan Christians in refugee resettlements soon realized that they had to take responsibility for the spiritual health of their own people or simply forget about it.

The Church inside Rwanda did nothing to reach out to the refugee churches outside the country. Nor did the churches in the refugee camps take it upon themselves to reach inside Rwanda, as such an effort would probably have been dangerous for those inside. Relationships would have been better if developed from the inside out, and at the initiation of key church leaders. The CPR (Council of Protestants in Rwanda) could have taken that initiative to make contacts with church denominations in the refugees' host countries. But the situation was left alone, and only individual contacts were made through international conferences, Christian gatherings and educational institutions around the world.

EIGHT

The Corruption of Church Leadership

WE HAVE INDICATED that church leaders' political involvement, close ties and relationships with government authorities contributed to the dearth of prophetic voices in the ethnic conflict that tore Rwanda asunder. Out seeking power, recognition and financial advantage, church leaders have been corrupted by the politicians with whom they associated. Usually, politicians have simply tried to gain church leaders' moral support to expand their own influence, and from the initial days of colonialism, Christian missions were too involved with the sociopolitical matters of the Rwandan kingdom and colonial administration.

The Catholic mission's dream was to establish a Christian kingdom in the central Africa region. The Catholic mission leaders, though, were once refuted by the German colonial leadership and asked to keep out of administrative business. The White Fathers had already engaged in criticizing the traditional Rwandan social structure, calling it an unjust oppression of the peasant Hutus, but neither was the colonial indirect rule what the White Fathers wished to see; they wanted a radical change of the traditional structure toward a European model of leadership. While the Protestant mission leaders kept low-key, but had the ear of the German colonial officials, the White Fathers were jealous of this relationship. Despite the Germans' reaction to the White Fathers' involvement with the Rwandan peasant population, and to their militant spirit to protect their newly converted, mainly Hutus, from Tutsi oppression and unjust practices, the priests continued their non-evangelistic role to expand their influence and popularity among the Hutus, thus compromising the biblical teachings of love and unity.

The Belgian colonial administration offered the White Fathers a different status, and close ties with the Belgian administration both within the country and in Belgium developed. The Catholic mission wasted no time in seizing pastoral opportunities and gaining political influence in the country, which they wanted to move towards being a Christian kingdom. The mission did not have to lobby hard for an influential position in the new colonial leadership; their language skills, Rwandan cultural understanding and popularity among peasant people earned them the colonial administrators' respect and opened a door for them as technical advisors. The administration heavily depended on the Catholic mission leaders, who took advantage of the situation not only for the work they initially set out to do, but also to influence political reforms they had long desired.

The Catholic mission together with the colonial administration became the most powerful institutions in the country. Each had a political agenda. The Catholic Church leadership was soon to lose its focus of pastoral work and church planting for a vision of political domination and the desire for Christian influence to permeate all aspects and levels of the Rwandan kingdom.

King Musinga rejected the Christian teaching of the White Fathers, and resisted the Belgian governmental approach that was moving away from the German-initiated 'indirect rule' toward the Belgian Congo colonial administration model. Both the Catholic mission and the colonial administration wanted to remove Musinga. The Catholic Church leadership hated the king because he was not willing to be baptized or to give up his many wives, while the Belgian administrators felt he was too much in the way of the political reforms they wished to see happen. To the colonial officials he was considered indifferent, while he was viewed as anti-European and anti-Catholic by the White Fathers. To both, he was a roadblock to European progress in Rwanda, so the two powers deposed Musinga and replaced him with his son king Rudahigwa. Before Rudahigwa's enthronement, four key men had been meeting to come to a 'colonial consensus' on a viable candidate to the throne: Bishop Classe, the deputy governor of the colonial administration, Mr Voisin and General Tilkens. Bishop Classe was entrusted with the responsibility of breaking the news to Rudahigwa regarding the change in leadership that they were about to make. Rudahigwa, then chief of Marangara, was also a Catholic Church adherent and a catechumen.

The deposition of the Rwandan king Musinga by both the colonial and Catholic Church administrations was the first *coup d'état* in Rwanda organized by Europeans. Whether the church leadership's involvement in the overthrow of one government and the establishment of a new one was within the church mission parameters is the key question. It is one that haunts me as a writer, as an observer of the situation, and above all as a Christian.

The successful replacement of the king led to continued Catholic Church involvement in politics. At the Church's initiative, the young king

Rudahigwa was baptized and given the name 'Charles', thus opening the door for royal Tutsis to follow in his footsteps. To the Catholic Church, the king's public acknowledgement of his Catholicism was a big triumph that helped them to gain even more influence in politics. Also, it suddenly made the White Fathers abandon the Hutus, whom they had supported for over 18 years in an effort to liberate them from the Tutsi oppression. The top Catholic leadership supported a discriminatory educational system which they ran and limited to children of the Tutsi chiefs and other nobles. Even though the Belgian colonial administration could be blamed for the same, the Church was in a position to refuse to operate schools under such a system. But this is no surprise, since the Catholic Church promoted racial superiority and held the Tutsi to be descendants of the North with Caucasian linkage, and therefore of higher intelligence – Bishop Classe first believed that without Tutsi leadership, the country was doomed to fall. The Church's political involvement in schools, social services, and in the public affairs of the country, continued until the 1950s: high-ranking church officials served on the king's court, and the church leadership model provided by the Catholic Church was later to be adopted by the national church leaders.

The second half of the 1950s became years of major political changes and upheavals in Rwanda. The result was a new government put in place by the influence of the two most powerful political powers in Rwanda: the Catholic Church and the Belgian administration.

For stability and proper establishment, the new Rwandan government needed the Catholic Church and its influence to propagate politics and policies. The Catholic Church had a tremendous influence in all parts of the country. Further, its publication *Kinyamateka* (founded by the White Fathers in 1933) was used by Kayibanda, the first Rwandan president, to sensitize Hutu readers to mass towards revolt against the Tutsi leadership. The Rwandan government needed the Catholic Church leadership more than that church needed the government. Most social services and educational institutions were in the hands of missionaries, and for public relations, both external and internal, the Rwandan government had no choice but to keep the close relationship with the Church that had spanned more than a quarter century.

By 1961, the Catholic Church was profoundly connected with the Hutu-dominant republics; Kayibanda's proclamation of the 'Country of the Battutu' received wide support from the Church, which knew that the government's aim was to promote Hutu solidarity against what it called

'Tutsi feudalism'. The identity card introduced by the colonial rule was retained and the Church said nothing about it. The newly formed government managed to use the Church for furthering much of what had been started and propagated through *Kinyamateka*, the White Fathers' journal. Favouritism and the prestigious position of both the Church and its leaders served to blind the Church. As the Burundi people's saying goes, '*Nta Umugabo uvugana irya mukanwa*', meaning 'No man talks with food in his mouth'. The favours and prestigious positions were used to manipulate the church leaders, who, for fear of losing these, could not address real issues. More than that, their ethnic identities came before their Christian beliefs and Christian identity.

The Protestant Church, on the other hand, was a minority and with little influence. Anglican missionaries had been associated with the Tutsis, and certain among them had actually crossed the border to Burundi to work with refugees. Protestant denominations had evangelists and some ordained pastors, but no key figureheads until the formation of the *Conseil Protestant du Rwanda* (CPR) in 1962. The CPR earned the Protestants a voice loud enough to be heard, and the development funds coming in from organizations such as the World Council of Churches and American-based mission agencies soon attracted government authorities. Generally speaking, the Protestants were less tainted with overt political involvement, though some denominations were quietly known as Hutu- or Tutsi-dominated. After the formation of the CPR, political manoeuvres started, and corruption found its way in. Foreign aid, money and development projects brought attention to the Protestant Church, elevating the CPR's position and recognition, and its leaders 'joined the club'.

The Protestant Church is not significantly mentioned in the histories of the sociopolitical conflicts of 1959–61 and 1972–3. By contrast, much has been written about the Catholic Church's role; and the Rwandan population, very much dependent on oral traditions, tells stories of the Catholic Church. One of the reasons the Catholic Church has been attributed with a significant role in the Rwandan conflicts was its provision of communication channels that were used to mobilize the general population. More than that, the first Rwandan president Kayibanda was a son of the Church and close to the hierarchical leadership that was committed to him and his political orientation. The Protestants, as we have noted, found their own ministry among the suffering. They helped refugees flee, especially those close to the Uganda border, and they hid certain individuals: the stand of the Protestant Church at that time gave them a position to help in the reuniting and reconciliation of the Rwandan people. They could have taken a strong, vocal stand as some did in the 1930s when missionaries (like those of the Anglican Church) challenged their church members to oppose the identification card. But perhaps the lack of numbers and of key educated leaders among the Protestants contributed to a feeling of inferiority that made them afraid to involve themselves in what would have seemed to human eyes a losing battle. Credit must be given to the East African Revival for producing a few God-fearing men and women known as 'The Saved', who condemned sinful acts among themselves, and among a few other small groups. God was still using some remnants and new converts of the East African disciples to witness and call sin by its name.

As Burundian people say, '*Ntamwonga ut a bura isato*', meaning 'There is no valley without a viper save where it has not been hunted.' There were older Catholic priests who sided with the Tutsi, but Hutu social democrats, mainly schoolteachers and seminarians, were able to use their positions to disseminate their ideas. I don't really know if the Rwandan Tutsi population can ever forgive Archbishop Perraudin, a Swiss White Father, who was a true militant for the Hutu revolution and saw it to its success at the price of the Rwandan citizens' blood.

In 1973, the Protestant Church was still unprepared to participate in the conflict or take a pastoral role. The missionaries had left by then, and Protestant church leaders were not courageous enough to stand up and speak against the evils of the Rwandan leadership and Hutu extremists' acts. Nothing had been done to address the Church's political involvement against the Tutsis in 1959–61, much less the public acts. This would not be the time either. Instead, Tutsi priests suspected by the government (or anyone else who wanted them to be killed) of having contacts with outside Rwandans were imprisoned. Others disappeared.

The 1973 massacres targeted schools, mainly because Tutsi Catholic priests had become successful in helping Tutsi students. Most Catholic institutions were dominated by Tutsi priests who had benefited from the early discriminatory school system of the colonial and Christian mission establishment. The Tutsi young people had no other place to go, but had to find a Tutsi leader who understood their fate. The government had made a decision to diminish job opportunities for them, and they were being expelled from schools, especially post-elementary schools.

The Hutu governments did what Kayibanda once accused the Tutsi of having done. In an interview with Ian Linden, Gregoire Kayibanda (then president of Rwanda) stated that while the Tutsis started out rejecting the

Church, they later embraced it and 'cornered it for themselves'.[1] The Catholic Church desired very much to turn Rwanda into a Christian kingdom, and so they involved themselves in the sociopolitical aspects of Rwandan affairs. They allowed the Church to be politically compliant to the regime, but later switched their allegiance to achieve their first desire. But even as Kayibanda indicated that the Church was being manipulated by the Tutsi for political purposes, it seems he used the Church to gain and maintain the leadership monopoly that constantly manoeuvred one group against the other.

I believe that the adoption of colonialism by the missionaries, the discrimination in schools, the deposing of the Rwandan king Musinga, and the political involvement and upheavals of 1959–61 all modelled the kind of behaviour and church leadership manoeuvres that threaten the Church's prophetic message. I think that the model provided to Rwandan Christians by the Christian colonial mission and the colonial administration was not that of solving conflicts and relations with the state; rather, the model showed how to co-opt conflict to one's advantage. Theologically, the Catholic Church had no grounds for political involvement in Rwanda from the very start to the 1950s and through 1961, let alone its continued involvement throughout the Habyarimana regime. The Catholic Church (and later the Protestant mission, for that matter) failed to address biblically the issues of racism and ethnic differences in Rwanda. Instead, most church leaders took advantage of the differences for their own glory and for political advancement of their ethnicity. Rwanda needs church leaders who can model true Christian testimony and leadership qualities.

The seating of the Roman Catholic Archbishop of Rwanda on the Central Committee of the ruling party of ex-President Habyarimana's government was like putting a stamp of approval on the politics and policies of a government that discriminated against its own people. The Archbishop's position and relationship to the government identified the Church with the position of the government on the social and political issues regarding the Tutsi population. It was the Catholic Archbishop who gave Protestant leaders tips on how to develop close relationships with political leaders. Some members of the Protestant churches (more so those of the Episcopal and Presbyterian), such as Bishop Sebununguri, Bishop Nshamihigo, Reverend Twagirayezu and others, made steps to develop relationships with Habyarimana, and came out in strong support of the man who gave them privileges and opened his living room to them. In later years the goal for many Christian church leaders, as they competed for relationships with Rwandan authorities, became clear. Each not only desired to be a close friend of the president, about which they bragged, but also sought to become a powerful voice of whatever church they were leading.

While I was still in my graduate programme, a top church leader from Rwanda visited my campus. My wife and I invited him over for dinner, and it was not long before we started talking about the Rwanda of my birth, but one in which I hadn't lived since the age of 4. This was in 1988. I was a student and stateless and the man felt sorry for me. He expressed that rather than me going back to Burundi or trying to find a country of second asylum, he would be more than happy to help me repatriate. I expressed fear for my life and clearly put it to him that since I left the country escaping machetes and spears for sins I did not commit, I was not going to go back to be killed by his government. The church leader, a bishop in his denomination, strongly stated that as long as he lived no one would touch me. He would offer protection. If I so wanted, he could call Rwanda's president (then Habyarimana) from my living room and ask him to send me amnesty papers and a passport. He further smiled and said, '*Yewe! Ntugire ubgoba! Hariya turishyikira,*' meaning, 'Don't worry and don't be afraid, we'll get to the top without any appointment.' The man scared me!

I actually thought that he was on a special mission, especially since it was right after the 1988 conference on Rwandan refugees held in Washington, DC under my chairmanship. I turned to my wife, looked in her face and communicated through facial expression. Verbally, I would have said, This man scares me! Who does he think he is? He will protect me! Only God can protect me and he knew better. So I furthered our conversation with the desire to learn more. I slowly asked, 'So, you mean bishops do not need an appointment to see the president?' He smiled and said, 'We just call and if he is home we drive over.' He stressed that he could see the president anytime he needed him as could some of the other bishops. He revealed an interesting thing in that conversation: 'A bishop's position is a political position,' he said. No wonder none could stand and speak prophetically in 1994.

Among the Protestant bishops, Episcopal Archbishop Nshamihigo and Bishop Sebununguri (even though some say that he had fallen out of grace with Habyarimana) were very close confidants of the president. Other bishops, such as Aron Ruhumuriza of the Free Methodists, were also in that circle of the president's 'living room friends'. Many sources have indicated that most church leaders had been bought off by the government officials through favours. The government's patronage of top church leaders had strings attached to it, and church leadership selection was one among many. Within the Rwandan Christian Church, among Protestants as well as Catholics, tensions always arose when there was an election or selection of church leaders. Scandalous situations and acts were observed more in the Episcopal Church of Rwanda. The selection of the very first bishop was a more political than spiritual matter. After dealings that were characterized by corruption and deceitful acts, the church ended up selecting a bishop based on ethnic criteria to satisfy the government's unwritten policy; the president of the country had to give his approval of the selection. Where ethnic distinction was not an issue for the top government authority, geographical origin could play a key factor, especially in the lay leadership of the Habyarimana regime.

While visiting Rwanda on my Compassion International responsibilities in 1993, I learned of a situation that typifies the church leadership selection practice. The Episcopal Church of Kigali Diocese had made a decision to open a new diocese in the Kibungo prefecture, home to the very first Episcopal (then Anglican) church established in Rwanda. The diocesan leadership, in the name of the Synod, met and discussed possible candidates. Finalists for the position were established and election held under the leadership and supervision of concerned individuals. Repeated twice, the election results came out in favour of Reverend Alfonse Karuhije, who was one of the very few Tutsi pastors of the diocese. (Reverend Karuhije was killed in the 1994 genocide.) The Episcopal Archbishop and others of his calibre contested the election and sought to enthrone a different candidate of their choice based on ethnicity.

Reverend Karuhije was threatened several times and asked to withdraw his candidacy as bishop-elect. According to my conversation with him while visiting Kigali in 1993, the Kigali diocese was divided on the issue. Bishop Sebununguri, then Bishop of Kigali and a close friend of the president, Habyarimana, was supportive of Rev. Karuhije and was the one who wanted to consecrate him. A number of Sebununguri's friends and canons were committed to the Karuhije side. Against the Rev. Karuhije's election were the Archbishop of Rwandan province, his royalists and the man he wanted to make Bishop (a Hutu, of course). The conflict went as far as it could go: to the president of the country. Both bishops were involved; Bishop Sebununguri and Archbishop Nshamihigo sought the president's help, each presenting his own candidate and reasons why the rival candidate should not be ordained. The then-president supported Archbishop

Nshamihigo against the electoral college's decision. Rev. Karuhije's disqualifying factor was his ethnicity, not his spiritual and Christian leadership qualities.

I was able to visit the Gahini parish five days before the actual ordination was supposed to take place. While at Gahini one of the key church leaders (and member of the electoral college) showed me a house that had been built for the new Bishop-to-be, Rev. Alfonse Karuhije. The original lock to the house had been replaced by the anti-Bishop-elect group, and the main entrance gate door was locked with chains. I was also told that a hit squad team had been organized and armed with machetes to kill Rev. Karuhije and whoever might turn up in an attempt to ordain him. Then-president Habyarimana had clearly stated that a Tutsi bishop could not be ordained. When Bishop Sebununguri approached him, taking advantage of the close relationship he had developed with the president over the years, the president told him that he could not do anything about it. He used Archbishop Nshamihigo as his scapegoat, although constitutionally, Archbishop Nshamihigo had no right to refuse a candidate elected by the diocesan synod outside his jurisdiction. A similar situation happened in the Catholic Church.

Rwandan Anglican bishops had vowed that a Tutsi could not be a bishop, except where the late Bishop Ndandali of Butare had ordained one for reasons advantageous to him. Bishop Ndandali was fighting to maintain the position of Archbishop now held by Nshamihigo. Realizing that he could not keep the position, he sought to divide the Church by ordaining new bishops and establishing a new province in which he would have continued to be the Archbishop. The man unconstitutionally 'established' a new diocese and ordained new bishops, one of whom was a Tutsi. He later made peace with the other bishops and legalized the ordination of the men he had chosen. Many key deacons and bishops in the Episcopal Church opposed the ordination of the one Tutsi bishop, whose life was subsequently threatened. The system was against him to such a degree that he had to give up his diocese and settle for being an assistant.

Nominations for any key church leadership position had to be informally approved by the president of the country. In most cases church leadership was not based on calling or spiritual and administrative qualifications, but on ethnicity and sometimes also the geographical area of one's origin. The Rwandan 'Ten Bishops in Seven Dioceses' system was built to accommodate tensions, but the scandals that hover over the background of the leadership conflicts are terrible.

It is no secret that the church leaders in Rwanda responded to two basic and related situations: the possible advantages of having extremely close ties to the colonial interests, and the pursuit of such ties with the first and the second Rwandan governments (the Kayibanda and Habyarimana regimes); these caused church leaders to compromise their prophetic and pastoral roles in exchange for being power-brokers of national politics.

NINE

Twilight of the Rwandan Church

WHEN THE CATHOLIC priests formally spoke out on ethnically sensitive issues in March 1990, it signalled a change in the thinking of the Catholic church leadership. The voices involved may not have been high enough in the hierarchy to be heard immediately as in past political involvements (such as those from 1916 to the 1960s), but they definitely provided a significant, if belated, warning. These priests spoke against the ethnic quotas in education and in civil service that limited Tutsi participation. Whether this was God's Spirit at work or the result of an intellectual analysis of the political situation (or both), I can't judge. Still, the warning should have been voiced at least some 30 years before. Given the clear signs leading to the climax of discriminatory and oppressive politics that was apparent both internally and externally, the country was at a crossroads: a choice of direction had to be made, or else there would follow the fall of the Habyarimana regime. The political agenda of 'Akazu', the circle of president Juvenal Habyarimana, had created enough enemies for the regime among southern Hutus, who were treated like second-class citizens under Habyarimana. Added to the discrimination against Tutsis in every aspect of the country's life, regionalism had become a basis of discrimination, so that Hutu discrimination and oppression against other Hutus was becoming unbearable and creating acute tension. Political scandals involving high government officials and members of the president's own family (more specifically on his wife's side) were rampant and included dealings that involved illegal currency, nepotism, the selling of gorilla babies and drug-trafficking.

Economically, the country was suffering from misuse of government funds, a food shortage in the southern part of the country and the collapse of world prices for coffee (Rwanda's main export). Meanwhile, the military budget for training, weapons and security was eating the country alive. Top military leaders helped themselves to the budget, hoping to match other politicians' financial status.

Externally, the 1988 Conference on Rwandan Refugees had been held in Washington. The conference raised issues regarding the Rwandan population in exile around the world, and declared the sole solution for Rwandan refugees was for them to return to their homeland. The conference agitated then-President Habyarimana, who immediately started political man-oeuvres. He requested that Rwandan refugee host countries offer the refugees naturalization or permanent residence. As noted earlier, his 'explanation' was that Rwanda was too small a country to accommodate everybody wishing to return. Discussions surrounding Rwandan refugees in the neighbouring countries of Burundi, Tanzania, Uganda and Zaire, however, applied great pressure to the Habyarimana regime. Habyar-imana's popularity was becoming history. He had political enemies both inside and outside the country and was basically ruling through a gun in his opponents' backs and 'suspicious' car accidents. The whereabouts of his identified enemies were top secret; human rights abuse had become a way of life, and his own conscience bothered him. For Habyarimana to think about Rwandan people in neighbouring Uganda had become an unbear-able pain for him and his entourage. Rwandan refugees in Uganda had experienced hardship and even expulsion under Obote.

The year of the five Catholic priests' circular on the subject of ethnic quotas in educational institutions and the civil service, 1990 was also the year of the Rwandan Patriotic Front's attack on Rwanda. Regardless of the letter and stand of the five priests, the majority of the Catholic leadership strongly supported the MNRD (Mouvement Révolutionnaire National pour le Développement), the then-president's political movement. After all, the archbishop had been a member of the Central Committee for over 20 years.

In 1991, one of the Catholic bishops again spoke publicly of ethnic dis-crimination in the country, challenging the Church's silence regarding the evil acts of the government. The pressure was on; fighting between the Rwandan Patriotic Front (RPF) and the then-Rwandan army continued, with each side claiming victories. The Rwandan army declared that the RPF was being pushed back into Uganda, even as the RPF claimed con-quered territories. The Rwandan army of the time discovered that they could not crush the RPF as they thought they would do, even with the help of countries like Zaire and France. The RPF was playing its cards carefully, tactfully and strategically, with the goal of gaining international recognition and minimizing losses in its army.

Under the pressure of the international community and local politics, Habyarimana bowed to political pluralism. Immediately, new political parties were formed, thus creating a forum for political expression. The political climate for the broadening of political parties was ripe, but the lack of political maturity was also apparent, as observed in local and inter-continental media. International media did report on significant happenings, but left out a lot of 'garbage politics' interesting to people with an understanding of the Rwandan political background. As political parties were formed and political orientations expressed, certain church leaders aligned themselves with the old political party of which some were already members, and others joined the newly formed parties. For church leaders who had befriended the authorities and received favours from them, it was now time to pay them back by showing the authorities strong support. They needed to rally their church members behind the patronizing former president, although there were a few who did not consider it wise as Christian leaders publicly to adhere to any of the political parties. The first year of political pluralism seemed to be interesting to everybody; politicization had already moved deep down into social structures and churches throughout the country. The issues of ethnicity and regional discrimination were alive and dominated political campaign platforms, Sunday sermons in some churches, and after-church talks in others. The spirits of Hutu extremists were running high and sounded everywhere in the country.

Fear of political failure and the growing unpopularity of the party in power engendered political assassinations, bombings, arrests, demonstrations, imprisonment, harassment, looting, extreme corruption and lawlessness in the country. Suddenly there was total insecurity in and around Rwanda. Slowly people started losing hope and respect for politicians and the political process as a whole; there were sporadic peace accord meetings, but fighting continued to claim lives, territory and a little more negotiating power: a military success would always serve to return a fighting faction to the negotiating table after a peace accord violation. There was also a certain desire among the international community's arbitrators to bring the conflict to an end, and so alleviate the suffering of innocent people both in and outside the country. Rwandans at home and in exile watched the situation with special interest and involvement – emotional, social, spiritual or political – at different levels.

The Christian community, both within the country and in the Rwandan refugees' host countries, followed developments with different reactions. In Rwanda, certain denominational leaders were close friends and strong supporters of the Habyarimana regime. Among them were all the bishops of the Episcopal Church of Rwanda (except one non-diocesan titular bishop formerly in Kigeme, a Tutsi and survivor of the genocide), the former president of the Presbyterian Church, the Free Methodist bishop, the Baptists' former leader, and all but two Catholic bishops. Some of the church leaders' reputations became widely blurred as they appeared in political scenes, advancing political agendas, leading political party demonstrations, and making inappropriate political declarations in public support of the corrupt regime – including the justification of both genocide and the mass killing of Hutu moderates. The Anglican leader Augustin Nshamihigo, the former Presbyterian head, and the Catholic Church's Archbishop Nsengiyumva acted like competitors. The silence and role of the top church officials during the 1994 massacres made them accomplices in the genocide.

Some church leaders (not in the categories mentioned above) and their followers were fed up with the nonsensical secular political games and lost confidence in their top leaders. Others became opportunists and sought to rally congregations of people behind them, but not necessarily with a commitment to the radical transformation of lives or an honest desire for peace and unity. For the opportunists, 'business-as-usual' church politics of position-seeking, the accumulation of material wealth, recognition and regionalism motivated their move toward gathering and holding Christian group meetings.

Some Christians around the world were disappointed in the Rwandan church leadership, while others were morally and financially behind them. From my discussions with executives of Western-based Christian non-government organizations and mission agencies, I have come to learn that many were confused and did not know what to believe about the Rwandan situation. So they continued their working relationships with churches and other indigenous Christian organizations in the country, based on the relationships and trust developed over the years prior to the 1990 war situation.

During this time, outside influence and counsel combined with certain church leaders' insights and led to an historical event. The All Africa Churches Conference (AACC) facilitated a church leadership meeting with the Rwandan Patriotic Front. Some people in East African church leadership claim that the meeting between the RPF and the Rwandan church leadership was influenced by Rwandan Tutsi nationals who were on staff with AACC at its Nairobi headquarters. This claim still remains to be substantiated. Before the conference held in Mombasa, Kenya, a joint meeting between well-meaning Catholic priests and certain Protestant church leaders had been held to discuss what could be done towards peace. The meeting actually produced a joint plea for peace. It was not long before they established a joint committee to continue interaction for peace with government officials, and to support peace efforts that were being made. Corruption, fear for life, job protection, and close ties between the top church leadership and the former president, worked together to kill the commission's efforts – a reality that further divided the Church through deep politicization.

The downing of the presidential plane and the start of the 1994 genocide accentuated the Church's silence and compliance. Individual bishops and other high-ranking church leaders dusted their suits, polished their shoes, wore their ministerial collars and took off on church-related 'missions' to raise funds, supposedly to help war victims. They 'explained' the Rwandan situation to the international community, targeting church-related circles. Such missions were conducted by the Archbishop of the Episcopal Church in Rwanda, Augustin Nshamihigo (among others), and with him Jonathan Ruhumuriza, Anglican Bishop of Kigali. While travelling and raising funds, they failed to condemn what was going on in Rwanda during the genocide but instead took a position that condemned the RPF and praised the interim government that was committing genocide. I was in Nairobi when two bishops of the Anglican Church called a press conference on their way to London. Journalists walked out of the room in disbelief at what they heard from the church leaders.

Honest Christians, godly people, the 'saved' (in the Kinyarwanda language, '*Abarokore*') were holding evening and weekend meetings characterized by groups engaging in prayer, fasting, confessions of sins, predictions of what might come, rich Bible studies, willingness to entertain deep thoughts, singing heavenly songs and concern for one another. Both Hutus and Tutsis participated with no fear of each other, even though there was an atmosphere of suspicion in the country. The meetings developed into large public gatherings where political issues were addressed, and the involvement of church leaders in the political scenes was condemned. There was a call to pray, to love each other and to pursue peace and unity. Christian survivors of the genocide who participated in these evangelical meetings tell stories of church members and testifying Christians who, having attended the same meetings, were later seen in the uniforms and activities of *Interahamwe* (militia). During the killings, many were also seen at roadblocks with machetes. It is hard to believe, but reported by trustworthy individuals. Equally, however, there are testimonies of godly people who lost their lives in the initial stages of genocide and mass killings of Hutu moderates, not because they were Tutsis, but as Hutus who spoke against the wishes of top church leaders and government officials.

Part Four

—

Bloody Sanctuaries

TEN

Hide, Kill or Point a Finger

SINCE THE 1994 holocaust in Rwanda, I have travelled for conferences, consultation work and my normal Compassion programme development activities in twelve countries on four continents besides North American cities. In these countries, the same question has been asked of me again and again: How did Christians behave during the killings?

I used to struggle in answering this question until I decided to address the same question to Christians who survived the genocide and hid within Rwanda from April to July 1994. These are individuals who lived at the heart of the situation.

The first answer to my question was from a friend of mine that I highly respect. His immediate response came through body language that said, 'Don't ask'. He then looked me in the face and said, 'Brother, you don't want to know!' I actually found out that some Christians (that is, church members) actually killed, while others hid long-standing close friends. There were yet others who could not pick up a machete, raise it up and kill someone, but who would point a finger to where a Tutsi was hiding. Quite often the untold story is of those ministers and lay people who stood firm to their faith and did their best to protect innocent victims. When I asked a more direct question such as 'Do you know a Christian who killed?' people would tend to speak in general terms, but there are some who can actually name a few church members they know who killed. It is said some of the killers wouldn't even deny the act, except in instances where they feared for their own survival. There are reports of Christians who have confessed killings, according to oral reports of people working in refugee camps. A close friend (whose name will be protected) said, 'What would you have done? You were told to kill or else you would be killed!' As he shared the story, I couldn't help but wonder if he had not participated or at least been around people who did it. Not leaving him alone, I revised the question to him and asked, 'Well, what would you have done?' He did not want to answer my question, but simply said, '*Umva data ku ubukristo bganyu bukomeye!*' ('Talk about your strong Christian stand').

Most Tutsis that I met and interacted with during my September 1993 visit to Kigali lived in great fear of what would happen if the Arusha Accord did not go through. I remember sitting in a hotel restaurant with a friend, who was killed in April 1994. He and his wife were terrified. Lists of Tutsis living in Kigali had been made; some had already been matched with people who would kill them if and when the plan was carried out. Church members were reported to be among the executors of the plan that had been drawn, and they were actively involved in the list-making.

It was not hard for me to believe most of what I heard while in Kigali, mainly because of stories I heard from my own family of the 1959–61 killings of Tutsis. While living in a refugee camp in Burundi, I used to hear people saying that catechumens who always attended churches were among the first to take up machetes in their hands and burn the houses of their Tutsi neighbours. Unfortunately, the same stories are told about church members in the 1994 slaughter. I could also remember hearing stories of the Episcopal Church fights involving the late Bishop Ndandali, Bishop Sebununguri and Archbishop Nshamihigo. There were serious fights where weapons were carried into meetings and special bodyguards hired on suspicion of life-threatening plans.

When Rwanda's former president died in 1994, the killing started within hours. The very evening the presidential plane went down and the news spread, Tutsis started searching for hiding-places. Some Tutsis had actually developed escape plans prior to what happened on 6 April, since the inevitability of an 'ethnic purge' had been made known. The orchestration of death and genocide was not an overnight plan, but a strategy that had been in the making for a number of years. People knew that it was not a matter of 'if', but instead a matter of 'when' it was going to happen. As in the 1959 situation, people hid in churches, on the roofs of their houses (or those of their Hutu friends), in bushes and in holes. They went from one place to another whenever they were sure it was safe to make the next move. Propaganda had sunk into the minds of people, and Radio Mille Collines called on Hutu extremists and militia to 'go to work' and 'finish the job'. They were told to take up anything that could be used as weapons. Militia had actually trained people in secret, and church young people had participated in the training with machetes, axes and iron bars.

The general behaviour of Christians during the 1994 genocide was not exemplary, even though there were heroes of faith as will be discussed in later chapters. Genocide survivors have shared stories of how people were killed and of who killed them. Among the killers were church members of both Catholic and Protestant faith. Of course, one wouldn't expect church leaders known for infighting to produce church members characterized by harmony and the unity of believers. When church leaders cannot model qualities of Christian living, especially those of unity, love and peace, in a context like that of Rwanda, they actually poison the congregation and hinder the spirit of God from working in the lives of those church members they lead. The behaviour model for church members, and for the Christian life of its congregation, should normally be demonstrated by its leaders.

While still commuting from Kabale, Uganda, into Rwanda for relief operations, I saw an older man at Byumba. This man looked lonely, and lost in his thoughts. He reminded me of an old Catholic priest I knew as a child in the refugee camp where I grew up. The old Catholic priest would walk with his hands behind his back reciting his prayers and sometimes talking to himself. To me (and other children in the camp) he was known as 'The Philosopher', and we always commented that it was because he had studied too much. We believed that if he was not careful, he might become mentally ill. And now, this older man in the Byumba camp for internally displaced people was walking exactly like him. I walked to where he was, hoping to comfort him. I had no doubt that many of his people had been wiped out by the killers. As I talked to him, I found out that he was indeed a Catholic priest. We started talking about faith and the Christian Church in Rwanda. He categorically mentioned to me that he was not going to go back into pastoral work even if the genocide stopped and peace was established again. I wanted to be sensitive to how he felt, so I asked him, 'Why?'

The priest had been disappointed by the behaviour of his own church members. He could not comprehend how people he had served for years, people some of whom he had baptized, people with whom he had shared 'fresh food and cooked' (to use his term), had become the people who wanted to kill him. God had saved him, but he was upset at the number of people that he personally knew from the church, on the roadblocks with machetes, iron bars and clubs, ready to kill. When I mentioned to him that I also was an ordained minister, the man looked at me in disbelief and wanted to know what I was doing. I explained to him my work with Compassion International, a ministry of holistic child development. His comment was that working with children was the best approach to solving Rwanda's future problems, but he strongly believed that only people who did not experience the genocide could do it. He believed that in order for the Church in Rwanda to regain credibility, new church leaders, new pastors and priests had to be elected. Further, the ministry approach had to be different, and how different he did not know.

Obviously, this man was highly traumatized, but there was truth in what he shared. The conflict and tensions that led to genocide also put Rwandan Christians' behaviour in a spotlight that clearly demonstrated what I have decided to call 'the Christian deficit of love'. The greatest commandment of loving your God and loving your neighbour as yourself did not appear to have made any impact on the lives of the great majority of Rwandan Christians.

To some church members (Christians) whose lives were in danger, churches, church halls, church schools and hospitals were thought of as 'safe' places to hide. The villages and countryside as a whole had become too small a place for the victims to hide. Roads were blocked, forests were being burned; basically, any possible hiding-place was being destroyed. In 1959 Christian institutions had become a place of refuge for many. Rarely were people killed at the church stations or even taken away to be killed. In the 1994 killings, people on the run thought in the same terms. Some ran to churches in their communities hoping that there they would be safe. But as we have seen, in most communities Tutsis had been identified since the 1990 RPF attack and put on 'hit lists'. In certain parts of the country they had been told that they would be wiped out in due course. Hutu militia and extremists in each community knew who their victims would be when the order was given, and when it did happen, the killers searched for those they were responsible for killing. The Hutu community was expected (and in some cases required) to locate and identify Tutsis. As a result, they either killed or pointed to the hiding-places of Tutsis on the list. Either out of fear of being killed or out of hatred, most Hutus did what was expected of them.

I have a friend whose parents were Christians with a strong historical involvement in the Church. The couple had survived the 1959 killings, and endured the humiliation, frustrations and hardship of the 1960s. Ethnic hatred barred them from serving in key positions of the Church, but they persisted and served faithfully where they could. When their time came in 1994, they were promised protection and were in fact encouraged to leave their home and go to the church for better protection from the church leadership. When most of the Tutsis in the area, the majority of whom were members of the church, had congregated inside and around the church compound, militia were called in by well-known church members to complete their task of killing. None of the Tutsis survived the killing.

Incidents such as those are often recounted in Rwanda. Most Hutus who did not want to kill had no choice but to support the killing or pay a high price. Non-compliance with what was viewed as 'the Hutu patriotic spirit' was viewed as a lack of 'patriotism'. I found out from Hutus that I met outside Rwanda that the killing of Hutu moderates was a lesson to whoever would not participate. The situation in Rwanda forced many Christians to exercise the biblical teaching 'Choose for yourselves this day whom you will serve' (Joshua 24.15). There were Christians who knew their identity in Christ, and chose to serve their Master. Some paid a high price for their Christian commitment and for decisions made based not on ethnic identity, but on Christian identity. Oneness in Christ! Stories are told of pastors and priests who encouraged the act of killing without mercy, saying that God had given the Tutsis up for death. I heard one stark example from a friend, the son of a Seventh Day Adventist pastor, who went to visit his home village from exile in Kenya, where he had fled in 1990. Arriving in his home town, he started enquiring about his rela-tives, only to find out that all of them had been massacred. Someone who approached him indicated that unbelievable acts of killing had taken place in the area. They mentioned the name of a pastor colleague of my friend's father, and how that pastor was leading a group of militants committed to kill with the slogan 'God gave them up, kill them without mercy' ('*Imana yarabatanze ni mubice ntambabazi*'). Nevertheless, some churches have given birth to the martyr when a pastor or a priest accepted death with his flock, or when both Hutu and Tutsi faithful, congregated in the church, refused to separate at the request of murderers wanting to kill only Tutsi. These Christians chose to die together rather than to betray their faith or profit from their ethnic origin.

Theologically, one could put this question to the Rwanda Christians: What does it mean to be 'a Christian' or 'the people of God' in your context? However, I feel that this question was, in practical terms, put before the Christian mission when it began in the country. The Christian mission that opened its activities in a then-stratified community, with a system of 'lords' and 'clients', had an opportunity to preach the gospel of love, unity and equality of men before their maker. Instead they chose to emphasize the superiority of one group over the other. As the Church grew, an excellent evangelistic effort was carried out by all mission agencies involved. Some churches modelled a mission theology based on ethnic divisions. The paradoxical stand of the Church, on issues of ethnicity, of collaboration and relationships with colonial powers, of Christian ethics, and of socioeconomic and political structures of the country, have all shaped the Christian Church in Rwanda. I feel the Rwandan people, though evangelized, still lack the biblical teaching to nurture them to be mature Christians who would have wisdom and the wherewithal to draw from in times of difficulties.

I will not hesitate to say that the Christian community in Rwanda, thanks to the traditional Rwandan educational model, learned from their church founders and leadership as a whole: they observed, imitated and participated. The conflicts, the political leanings, the emphasis on one ethnic group, and the mishandling of controversies, are not new in the Rwandan church. But the problem is that the Church refused to resolve conflict and contradiction. They chose instead to take the path of least resistance and avoid controversy. For some church members, the genocide and mass killing of moderates provided an opportunity to express and put into action what had been inwardly suppressed. How the Christian mission and the Church in Rwanda understood what it meant (and what it means) to be 'a Christian' and 'the people of God' is a question that could be explored more.

In hope that their children could escape the carnage, some Tutsis left them with Hutu friends. Many of those Hutus abandoned the children for reasons that ranged from belief in the propaganda to fear that if they were found with Tutsi children they would be killed. In previous mass Tutsi killings (in 1959, 1963 and 1973) children, women and elderly people were not killed. In fact Tutsi women were often taken in marriage, although others were raped or left alone. In 1994, many women were raped and killed irrespective of age. Babies, children, elderly, and even severely handicapped Tutsis were killed. My grandfather, one such, was 83 years of age. The killers were determined to exterminate every Tutsi, so that in future, a Hutu child would have to ask what a Tutsi looked like.

While many went to the churches for refuge, others sought refuge among fellow church members and long-standing friends; and there were individuals who hid friends until it was safe for them to emerge. Again, stories of such heroes are not often told, but I hope to discuss some in the chapters ahead, and I must share one such story now.

Immediately following the takeover of the capital city and most of the rest of the country by RPF, I was appointed as Acting Country Director for Compassion International, with a mission to continue the relief assistance programme we had started and to re-establish Compassion's child development work in the country. I was busy in my office when a man was introduced to me as a potential employee. I spent time with him and decided to give him an application form as I walked him out of my office. Shortly after he left, one of the people in the office revealed to me that the particular individual who had just left had an interesting story that I needed to hear. The man had 'seen it all', but most of all he had saved lives. I was told that he hid people in his house and helped them to escape to safety. As things progressed and people started trickling into Rwanda from outside the country, as well as in camps for internally displaced people, I kept hearing stories such as his. Meeting him again was a blessing. I thanked him and thanked God for his noble courageous action in the most difficult times. The man was quick to admit that he was able to act that way only by God's grace, and continued to express the view that Rwanda was divided for the selfish reasons of colonialists. Amazingly enough, he observed that the hatred and divisions were also modelled for us in the Church.

The behaviour of the Christian community in Rwanda generally disappointed the worldwide Christian community. However, Christians around the world need to admit that similar situations, though not exactly the same as in the Rwandan context, exist around us. The challenge that we have as believers is to work out our understanding of what it means to be 'Christians' or 'the people of God' in our multiethnic environment. How we relate and behave is very important. Many times we are faced, as was Joshua, with the choice of whom we will serve.

ELEVEN

Bloody Sanctuaries, Silent Leaders

I HAD VISITED the country for two weeks in late September and early October 1993, but after 35 years in exile, my 1994 entrance into the northern part of Rwanda through Uganda was an emotional mixture of homecoming and grief. As we stopped for the immigration and security check on the Uganda side of the border, my eyes were looking over the mountains and across the bordering river. The process was quick, and I soon found myself on the other side after a short drive through the 'no man's land'. There I found RPF soldiers, young and dedicated. I wanted to hug them and kiss the land, but I was much too occupied by thoughts of what they had gone through. I wanted to ask them about my own younger brother, but I did not know where to start.

I greeted them in Kinyarwanda and immediately established relationships that allowed me to start asking questions. I learned that the RPF was controlling quite a distance from where we were, and that it was somehow safe in the area, though there were militia activities in certain parts of the Byumba prefecture. Without spending much time at the first roadblock, my team and I were sent to the next checkpoint. There I found acquaintances, but it wasn't until after I had been checked that a lady at the checkpoint raised her head and mentioned that she knew me. Within a short time, we were given an escort and were on our way to different camps of internally displaced people. On the way to Kibungo (south-east toward the Tanzanian border), I saw my first disturbing church scene.

The place was Kabarodo, a small town at an important junction leading off to the famous tourist Hotel Akagera. Our escort pointed out a church building with a huge hole in one of the doors. The second door was standing wide open. We had heard that people had been butchered in the church sanctuaries. A colleague and I decided to stop and take a look in the church. As we got out of the car, we were hit by the strong smell of decomposed bodies from behind the church. Our escort, in a quiet voice, turned to me and said, 'A thousand people were killed in this church.' We took care where we walked, picking up and comparing bullet shells, and we finally got to the church doors. The sanctuary was covered by a sticky dark layer of blood. The podium had been hit by a rocket and was overlaid with thick blood. As I walked around over little benches to avoid stepping in the semi-dry blood, I saw remnants of food, pieces of clothing and other small objects. According to the story provided by our escort, both Tutsis and Hutus were hiding in the church together, terrified and traumatized by the killings that were going on. *Interahamwe* (militia) came and separated the two groups, sending Hutus away back to their homes while they killed all the Tutsis in the church with grenades.

We drove off from the scene and continued our journey to Kibungo. The Catholic parish of Kibungo had experienced massacres and merciless killing. People in the community of Kibungo, especially Tutsis, had congregated at the parish church, but government soldiers and militia attacked the church, killing hundreds of people with grenades and machetes. Survivors were later helped by RPF soldiers and transported to where the RPF had established shelters for them.

Not far from the Kibungo parish in the same prefecture, we were told of the parish of Nyarubuye. The parish has been visited by most dignitaries, including the Archbishop of Canterbury, who have been in Rwanda since the genocide. An estimated 5,000 people were killed at this particular church. Bodies were everywhere; the church building had been packed to its maximum, and there were many others on the parish compound at the time of the killing. The militia, accompanied by soldiers, killed everyone in sight and were exhausted before they finished their killing task, which took a good two days. Even though there are many sites where people were massacred by the hundreds and even thousands, Nyarubuye will never be forgotten in Rwanda's history.

What I had seen and heard was enough for the day. I remember one of my colleagues called my name and asked how I was doing. He could not understand why I was not more visibly upset. He challenged me and wondered aloud why I was not grieving. He was concerned that I was taking everything inside and playing a macho-man on the outside. He did not think that I was being honest with myself and in my relationships with Hutus that I met, especially thinking of those who were on our staff. The truth was that I had not had time to grieve, even though I personally had lost distant relatives and friends. I was there for the relief effort, and I was committed to the mission that took me in. Once in a while, I did entertain ideas and thoughts of what the Hutus had done to my people, realizing how much they hated us, and wondering if we could ever live in harmony. Whenever we were not talking in the car, I was preoccupied by thoughts of how to help Rwandan people to learn to live together in peace as citizens of one country. I did not want to listen to people who believed that the solution to Rwanda's conflict would be to separate my people and have Burundian and Rwandan Hutus live together in one country, while the two countries' Tutsis lived in the other. I thought of what it would take to minister to both groups spiritually. And as I thought about that I couldn't help but think of the Rwandan church leaders I had met outside Rwanda, among them individuals I highly respected as spiritual leaders – suddenly my respect for them grew.

On our way back to Kabale, Uganda, from where most relief agencies were commuting, I wanted to stop in Gahini to see what the church station had become. Gahini, the birthplace of the East Africa Revival, was a significant station in the history of East African Christianity. I was curious about what I would learn and experience at the station. In September of 1993, I had visited the Gahini Episcopal parish. Fights for power and position among church leaders had rocked the church at that time. Divisions had arisen over the election of the diocesan bishop of Kibungo, who was stationed at Gahini, and the result was tension between Tutsi and Hutu church members there. As we drove to Gahini, we passed signs of destruction, tired-looking individuals, and wounded children, women and men on their way to the church hospital. Talking to a few individuals, I learned that people had been refused refuge in the church by one of the local pastors. Tutsi patients, and others who had sought refuge in the church hospital, had been taken out and killed. Well-meaning people had tried to help and failed, largely due to the church leadership and local authorities – among those who had tried to help save lives was a British medical doctor.

Rwanda now has a history of bloody sanctuaries; pastors, influential lay people and top denominational leaders were often implicated in the tragedies. The Church as an institution has failed the people of Rwanda from its very beginning; the role the Christian mission played in the country's early development cannot be ignored. While much of it can be applauded for the creation of schools and establishment of medical services, the role played by Christian mission leaders in colonial days and that of the church leaders after colonialism is, however, regrettable. The distinction between the church leadership of 1959–61 and that of 1994 is that during the 1959 massacres, church leaders did not allow murders in their sanctuaries, but rather allowed the Church to remain a place of refuge. In 1994, the Church became a slaughterhouse for thousands of people.

In my evaluation and analysis of the situation, two factors contributed to the slaughter in the Church: the Church–state relationship, and the Church's moral support of prejudice and impunity. During the Belgian colonial rule, the Catholic Church and the Belgians established and developed relationships that involved the Church in the leadership selection intended to replace traditional village leaders with professing Catholic Christians. The Church continued to involve itself in political issues based largely on ethnic distinctions, and sometimes gave birth to social injustices that equalled or dwarfed those it was trying to combat. The 1959 political revolution that produced the massacres of Tutsis was also an act of close collaboration between the Catholic Church, the élite militant Hutus and the Belgian colonial administration. Following this, the lack of will among top church leaders to speak out in confession on behalf of the Church was compounded by their lack of discernment and ability to distance themselves from an impunity that would contribute to the loss of a credible prophetic voice. Church leaders modelled no fear of God; their lives contradicted their biblical teachings; they contributed to the general population's disrespect and, therefore, to the undermining of the Church's moral authority and role in the community.

The Church in Rwanda supported political moves that always favoured one group of people against the other. Though the relational links between top church leadership and high-ranking government officials were beyond the everyday experience of the average Rwandan, the top church leaders represented the Church and the Church's stand on issues. In the past, Rwandans were never encouraged to challenge authority and question what they thought to be wrong, especially in the Church. So one can simply say that Christians in Rwanda are products of the kind of church leadership they had.

If one really takes a close look at the lifestyles of church leaders, a corollary can be observed in the members. If church members in Rwanda are to follow the examples of their leaders, and to this point many have, there is no reason to expect any behaviour other than that which was demonstrated in the 1994 genocide: church leaders were functioning as their own government, whose intentions were to exterminate members of their congregations, and they led multitudes of their followers down that path. African Rights has done well in documenting the priests and pastors who killed or encouraged killings.[1] Most of the clergy accused of killing and inciting people to kill are Catholic priests and Protestant pastors, including top church leaders, many of the accused having been in the southern and western part of the country, in the prefectures of Kibuye and Gikongoro.

How can the Church in Rwanda pretend to want to minister and be a spiritual support to a population they betrayed? It is a question I hear from many people. Miraculously, churches in Rwanda are packed today, as they were from the very first week the RPF took over leadership in Rwanda. I remember visiting people who would state that they wanted to go to church to worship, but did not want to see the church leaders who either participated in the killing or failed to condemn it as it happened. And although most church leaders have ignored the accusations against them and continued church business as usual, some have experienced strong opposition that has led to church division. The leaders concerned seem not to care, but continue to impose their leadership. Cash payments and in-kind gifts have been used to win over opponents, but the struggle continues; one would hope to see the leaders model another style and establish new principles of church leadership, but such instances are rare.

The silence of both Catholic and Protestant leaders has contributed to the general failure of the Church and the crisis in church leadership.

TWELVE

Where Was God?

'WHERE WAS GOD?' was the question of the hour as Rwandans began processing the horrors of the 1994 massacres.

It was not hard for me, as a Christian, to sit and listen to brothers and sisters in Christ give testimonies of God's greatness and mercy: they attributed their survival to God's doing, not their own. They were, however, disappointed by the behaviour of many church members they had known, before the hard times, and even during the months prior to the downing of the presidential plane that triggered the implementation of the planned extermination of Tutsis by Habyarimana's gang. As McCullum reported: 'By the time the presidential jet was shot down, the situation in Rwanda had become so explosive that the killings began in less than an hour, indicating the level of preparedness for the terror which was to ensue.'[1] Most Christians believed their top church leaders knew of the extermination plan. They were disappointed that none of those leaders did anything to defuse the situation, or even to counsel the President, who many of them – both Catholic and Protestant leaders alike – counted as a close friend. Even more, they were disappointed that church leaders made no effort to protect their flocks.

Relating to non-Christians, even to those seekers who attended church, was different and more difficult. They were angry at God in their grief and sorrows. They questioned (and some still question) God's love. They wondered where he was during the genocide. Rwandans had a common saying: 'God spends the day somewhere else, but spends the night in Rwanda' ('Imana yirirwa ahandi Igataha I Rwanda'). To many, God left Rwanda on 6 April 1994 and did not come back until the final defeat of the Rwandan army by the RPF soldiers.

But it was not only the non-Christians who were angry at God – many Christians were, too, and expressed it through attitudes of despair and hopelessness over the situation. I found myself asking why God did not intervene before thousands were slaughtered, but God is not responsible for our acts of sin. His intervention is always timely; it is just that our concept of time is different from his concept of time. Scriptures tell us,

'With the Lord a day is like a thousand years, and a thousand years are like a day' (2 Peter 3.8). God stands above time and sees time in terms of eternity.

There was a profound question among those often asked by most Rwandans after they had observed the roles of the top church leaders, individual pastors and priests. The question was, 'Will they stand up before people and preach again? If they do, who will listen to them?' The former government leaders' credibility had been lost; a new government was in the process of being established on new grounds. What about the leadership of the Church that had lost credibility and been tainted by their close links to the master planners of the genocide? What about their public stands and public addresses in support of the acts of evil against one group of people who made up part of their congregations?

A friend of mine laughed hard as we were discussing the situation. He made me reflect on statements often made in evangelical Christian circles that use language like 'God told me' and attributing our action to 'God's will'. His comment turned around the fact that some church leaders, pastors and regional presidents of certain denominations had incited people to slaughter others using the name of God. According to their words, 'God has given the Tutsis up!' The question is, did those who carried out the acts of killing under such incitement see themselves as accomplishing God's mission? It is a painful example of how certain church leaders or pastors can mislead people by uttering 'God told me' and 'This is God's will'. My friend was rightly noting the irony of using 'God-language' to incite atrocities. Church leaders had gone too far in doing everything they could to justify their actions.

The total victory of the RPF brought new life to Kigali, despite the signs of destruction, the smell of decomposed bodies, the grabbing of properties and the looting of goods left by the fleeing population. The caution employed by Rwandans (and the RPF soldiers in particular) to avoid dangerous traps as they sought to bring law and order to the ruins of Kigali offered new hope to the survivors of the genocide. People were flocking to Kigali from within the country, from neighbouring countries and from other parts of the globe, representing different missions, objectives and goals. However, all had one thing in common: they wanted to hear the stories survivors had to tell. To this day, different people approach the survivors' stories from different angles. The Rwandan population of 1959 refugees comforted 1994 survivors while they enquired about relatives and friends. Survivors searched for remains of their family members and friends, and for traces of other survivors. International media and human rights groups were in to investigate alleged human rights abuses of the past and present. Different non-government organizations and UN agencies were busily involved in humanitarian emergency relief work, as well as the re-establishment of any work in Rwanda they had supported before 6 April, and that included the search for any survivors among their former employees.

As I drove into Kigali shortly after the RPF victory, I was amazed by the people and faces I saw. It was overwhelming for me. I was meeting people I had not seen for years. Among these were young people who had joined the RPF while I was at graduate school in the United States, having left Burundi for America in 1984, and not returning until 1990. By then, many young people I knew had joined the movement. I also saw thousands of people (some of whom I knew) from the Rwandan refugee community around the world. These were people and descendants of the 1959 Rwandan refugee group. Hugging, shaking hands, shedding tears, shouting victorious words, welcoming and sweet reunion characterized the interpersonal reactions and relationships in the city. Driving in Kigali, I found myself stopping several times to hug and shake hands with people.

My first visit in Kigali after the RPF secured it was to a family who survived the genocide. Later, I took a ride with them in the suburbs of Kigali. The experience brought tears to my eyes, gave me a picture of the genocide and brought many memories to life. As my colleagues and I sat in the couple's house and listened, we were amazed by the story they had to tell. It was apparent to them that the genocide had been planned well in advance, although they did not know the day and the hour. Although the Arusha negotiations and accord had contributed to what many viewed as a possible alternative to conflict, certain former Rwandan government officials knew better. I learned from many informants, including Hutu friends, that some of the ex-government thinking was to promote power-sharing with the RPF, let them come into the country and then strategically eliminate them. The ex-president and his entourage of family members (especially his wife Agathe) had previously engaged in repression and political assassinations. There existed a group known as 'The Squadron of Death', which had been prepared and commissioned to protect the Habyarimana regime against any group of people, regardless of who they were. The target was not only the RPF, but anybody who sought to challenge the regime. The RPF were on two counts a major target for Habyarimana: that of being a majority Tutsi group, and that of being against Habyarimana. The Squadron of Death or 'Network Zero' (a term used by Hugh McCullum) was used to train killers and distribute arms.[2] The systematic execution of Habyarimana's political opponents was another indication of a well-planned catastrophe. Missionary friends and other expatriates who lived in the country tended to think that genocide was the result of the fighting between the RPF and the ex-government, and more specifically a fight between Tutsis and Hutus. But make no mistake: this was a well-programmed genocide.

Diplomatic missions in the country, UN agencies, church organizations and other non-government organizations knew about the Habyarimana regime's activities and plans against Tutsis, but Habyarimana had managed to make people believe that the RPF attack manned in October 1990 was a mission to reimpose a Tutsi autocracy on Rwanda. The picture that the colonial powers painted against Tutsis combined with the support Habyarimana received from his best friend in France, former President Francois Mitterrand, to ensure that no outsiders paid attention. The popular 'bottom line' was that no Tutsi could be trusted. This had gone too far in Rwanda. I personally know missionaries who clearly state that Tutsis cannot be trusted. I have had to suffer that perception as a Christian and have experienced it firsthand. The interesting part is that after I reached a stage where I did not need the missionaries, they trusted me and even tried to develop close relationships with me. They had turned around, saying to me that there were some Tutsis who were consistent in their behaviour and could be trusted.

Our host couple, that evening in Kigali, had been in hiding for 89 days. Sitting and listening to both share their experiences, and those of their children, was a blessing and a testimony to God's power. Every day of their hiding brought them close to being killed, but God chose to protect them. They testified to God's answering of their prayers and miraculous provision for their needs. God's protection and provision was not unique to them, but to many other survivors as well.

The common question to the survivors was 'How did you survive?' In most survival stories, God's name was mentioned in saying, '*Habaye ahi Imana,*' meaning 'It was only by God's grace,' or '*Ibyi Imana ikora n' ibitanga,*' meaning 'What God does is miraculous.' Many acknowledged God as the one who saved them, and Christian survivors shared stories of how believers they knew died praying, singing or sharing their testimonies with their killers. A friend I spent much time with indicated that there were not many survivors, but that the majority of those who survived did not survive because of their executor's forgiveness, but only by God's grace –

and they know that. Even though many may have asked where God was, many can also testify to his mercy.

The majority of Christian victims were killed in churches. Those who survived church slaughters testify that the victims often spent time in prayer and adoration. They gave their lives to Christ and died. Survivors also testify that there are those who died praying for their executors. Others recount that they knew of friends who, buried alive, were still singing until ground dirt engulfed them. Others thrown in pits sang and prayed until they surrendered their souls. Many Christians believe that God saved them for a purpose; in fact, many believe that God wanted them to remain as witnesses of his faithfulness and grace.

The most touching experience was to see and hear survivors sharing their stories with each other. They hugged and screamed as they saw each other. Many could not believe their eyes. They questioned each other to find out how they survived, they asked about friends and often broke out in tears as they talked about the darkest moments of their lives. They talked about the roadblocks and either explained or showed where they were. The roadblocks permitted the militia to check people's identity cards in an effort to single out Tutsis. Identified Tutsis were killed on the spot and their bodies thrown on the roadside awaiting the dump truck to take them to prepared mass graves. Tutsis' houses in the communities were destroyed, and their belongings taken. Tutsis found in homes were first asked to give whatever money they might have. Depending on the killers, some would take the money and go; others would take whatever they could, kill the victims and go.

The killing was competitive. People bragged about how many they had killed. Horrible stories were told about the killing. Sometimes, killers would have their victims kill their own family members before they were themselves killed. Children were made to watch the killings of their own parents; parents observed the killings of their children. Inhuman acts were conducted including the burning of victims to death, burying people alive leaving only the head exposed, and herding thousands of people into churches, sealing the doors, and then launching grenades and bombs into their midst from the outside.

The killers were encouraged to continue their work through several means. Radios, speeches by government officials and public rallies kept the inner fire burning; supplies of the necessary weapons kept them active. Survivors observed devilish acts and satanic worship in practices devised to prevent the victims' spirits from haunting the killers; and as killers moved from cities to villages, from valleys to mountains, the slogan was the same: 'Don't stop until the task is finished.' The Tutsi–Hutu hatred was being spewed out on the radio while Tutsi bodies were decomposing, strewn throughout the country. Hutus had 'learned' from the colonialists that Tutsis came from the north, probably Ethiopia, and as they threw bodies in the rivers they talked about 'sending the Tutsis back home'.

Most survivors I met were highly traumatized. They whispered as they talked, and did not know who to trust. As they saw Hutus they knew, they tended to want to hide. I remember driving with the previously mentioned couple in one of the Kigali suburbs. The wife saw someone she knew and screamed. She literally tried to hide her face by bowing her head down in the car to her lap. The husband did not want to look at the man they knew and also screamed while saying '*Interahamwe*!' Any reminder of the experiences they went through was a traumatic experience for the survivors. Many did not want to see people carrying machetes (or any other type of weapon, for that matter). Some survivors saw people they had seen on the roadblocks, in militia uniforms or at militia rallies. They saw people who had killed, and sometimes those who had victimized their own relatives. In the initial days after the RPF arrived in Kigali, there were many militia in the city who desperately hoped they wouldn't be found out. There were even some ex-government soldiers who had taken off their uniforms and tried to act as civilians.

I remember right in the city centre, near the commercial bank, a man who was believed to be an ex-soldier was being questioned by an RPF soldier. Rather than answering, he grabbed the gun of the young soldier who was questioning him and shot him. Though Hutus and Tutsis who knew each other shook hands and hugged in joyous disbelief at seeing each other, there was still much going on in the mind of every Rwandan.

Part Five

—

Scars and Healing

THIRTEEN

Fear, Shame and Joy

BY LATE 1994 in the streets of Kigali the repatriating Rwandan population and the RPF soldiers walked tall, though the situation and circumstances were difficult. Some enjoyed a sense of homecoming after thirty-five years in exile, where many had lived a very difficult refugee life. For others it was their very first time in the country of their ancestors. There is also a sense in which the RPF victory was a victory for all Rwandans of good will. Previous governments had oppressed and discriminated against even those with whom it had worked to eliminate the Tutsis in 1959. From the 1980s on, it had become obvious that the problem of Rwanda was not the Tutsis of 1959 and before, but bad leadership.

The Hutus, especially those who had been very vocal and active prior to the starting of the actual 1994 genocide, have been fearful. Those accused and proven to have participated in the killings have been rounded up and are now in prisons awaiting the international tribunal to commence its activities. Some Hutus were caught off guard, and did not get a chance to flee the country. Others were taken by surprise: they did not believe the country would fall to the RPF, due to the propaganda of the interim government of Sindikubgabo. Propaganda aired on government radio kept insulting the RPF, inciting people to kill, and lying to the population that they were still in control when in reality they were losing to the RPF. The ex-government that was moving from one geographical area to the other maintained a military presence in Kigali, the capital city, but the military was very cut off from the rest of the country by the RPF, who provided them a way out to minimize losses on both sides. The defeat surprised many militia and Hutus who were not aware of how the RPF was advancing. When the ex-army decided to run toward the Zaire border via Ruhengeri, many civilians were left in Kigali.

Watching the encounters between Tutsi survivors of the genocide and Hutus who knew each other – and knew the background and activities that prepared the genocide – was sad, yet interesting. While visiting the suburb of Gikondo within the first weeks of the RPF's victory that took Kigali, two friends and I were walking towards a destroyed house. The house belonged to a Tutsi, a brother of one of the friends walking with me. Coming our way was a Hutu Christian man familiar with both of my friends. The man did not expect them to be walking in the streets of Kigali. In fact when he saw them, he was shocked, as he expressed it, and thought that he was seeing their ghosts. The three hugged as I was looking, and at my turn, I shook his hand. I was introduced to the man, who looked at me and actually said, 'Is this Mbanda whose name I have always heard?' I observed them talking and sharing stories; the man was very uncomfortable, and did nothing but utter condemnations of the murders. He kept on narrating what they were going through as result and consequences of their evil acts. He was ready to reveal names of the murderers to anybody who wanted to know them. He thought that the new government should pursue them and bring them to justice regardless of how many years that may take. I can't stress enough how uncomfortable and how embarrassed the man was. He could hardly look anybody in the face, and kept wondering and wanting to know what action the new government was going to take. The two friends listened carefully. Once in a while they gave feedback that simply expressed their happiness and joy to be alive. They emphasized the greatness of God, and kept asking their Hutu friend what he thought when he saw them. Rather than answering their questions, he asked about other people they knew in common. Most of them had been killed. His response was that he did not expect them to be alive. I experienced many situations like the above story. In most cases, I observed palpable expressions that ranged from dismay, discomfort and regret, to a sense of relief, delight and certainty.

The coming out of hiding of both moderate Hutus and Tutsi survivors, and also the arrival into Kigali of those Tutsis who had been rescued by the RPF, made many Hutus nervous. The survivors could not help but wonder what part a Hutu might have had in the genocide. It is true that there are many Hutus who did not participate in the killing of Tutsis or Hutu moderates. Still, in situations like Rwanda's, it is not unusual for people to suspect each other. General distrust is a normal reaction until people start to communicate with each other. Most Hutus were suspected of being participants, just as most Tutsis were suspected of being '*Inkotanyi*' (RPF movement members). The Hutus felt guilty, and Tutsis felt like victims of the Hutus' well-planned genocide.

Guilt is the result of a violated moral standard held by an individual who feels responsible for that violation. The guilt felt by the Hutus can be classified in two different categories: the guilt caused by participation in action, and guilt felt by association. Both kinds of guilt spark fear of what the consequences might be, especially in the Rwandan situation where the genocide and victimization of moderate Hutus was stopped through a military victory. Many Hutus, both inside and outside Rwanda, believed that revenge was compulsory. The whole international community, including the relief and development agencies working inside Rwanda, expected to see acts of revenge throughout the country. If anything, the new Rwandan government has done a superb job in preventing such acts. For individuals who have tried to exact revenge, exemplary and severe penalties have been carried out.

The government is still working hard to bring unity and security to Rwanda. People who have done nothing to implicate themselves in the killings do not have to worry; it is those who are guilty of participation in the killings who should be – and are – uncomfortable. Unfortunately, there is nothing that can be done at this point to help innocent people except to ease their sense of culpability; and the only way to do that is through justice. Guilt by association may have to be eased by bringing justice to those accused of involvement. Justice will provide relief to those who are waiting and wondering what will happen to them.

The situation and atmosphere in Kigali was not the most pleasant and comfortable for the majority of Hutus in the country, who had observed the whole killing situation. Many stayed in their homes for days after the RPF established their presence in Kigali; others came out shameful of what their group had done to the Tutsi community. They were not sure what to expect. Many were fearful that the Tutsis might want revenge. At that time, I was actually commuting into Rwanda from Nairobi where my family lived. Nairobi was home to many Hutu refugees, militia and ex-government soldiers and officials. Those Hutus who dared talk about their feelings sounded fearful! They were not confident that Tutsis would not take revenge. The same fear was felt among the Hutus in Rwanda except that they were not free to express their feelings. Letters going out to their friends or people with whom they had contact outside did express fear of what might happen. Tutsis who had close contacts with those Hutus who remained in the country reported fear among the Hutu community in general. They were afraid either that the Tutsi survivors who knew about them would report their roles and involvement in the previous govern-ment's activities, or that the RPF would arrest them and question them about their Hutu friends not in the country but who might have been involved in the genocide.

Suspicion characterized Tutsi–Hutu relationships in the initial stages of the 1994 resettling in Kigali. Even a casual observer could sense the lack of trust in job-hunting, in relief activities, in government offices and even in public places.

I remember the talk and worry among non-government organizations that Tutsi employers would want to hire Tutsis and not employ Hutus. Most organizations were looking for Hutus to hire, because they felt that Tutsi would have all kinds of possibilities with the new government while the Hutus would be oppressed and probably harassed for the acts of genocide. Most organizations, including Christian NGOs, did not trust Tutsis. They had believed many of 'the old teachings' about the Tutsis coming to impose an autocracy on Rwanda. They were also led to believe that there would be revenge of some sort. NGOs looked out for the Hutus and sympathized with them. Many did not even pay attention to the genocide's survivors and what they had gone through. While looking for jobs, Hutus tended to go where employers were Hutus, Tutsis to Tutsis, and both to expatriate employers who sympathized with them. Tutsi employers were having a hard time finding qualified employees. Qualified Hutus would not come to them, afraid that they would be considered *Interahamwe*, since the general belief was that the majority of the Hutu population participated. The most difficult exercise for non-government organizations that did not want to hire Tutsis was to try to identify who was Tutsi and who was Hutu, since the physical characteristics imposed by the West do not apply any more. Most organizations hired employees and delivered relief supplies on the basis of ethnicity. The conduct of such NGOs and their practices only emphasized the divisions that had torn the country to pieces. Their action contributed to isolation and continued fear.

I remember a person who applied for a job I had advertised through Rwandan church leaders. One of the bishops recommended a person whom I found to be highly qualified for the job after two interview sessions, and I made an offer. The offer I made was attractive to this person, but her response was that she wanted to think about it, seek advice and then get back to me. Three days went by and I decided to contact her. To my disappointment, she refused my offer. I couldn't understand why she wouldn't take the job, given the package offered to her and the fact that she was making much less than was offered to her. Further, she had taken the initiative on her own to apply. After she turned down the offer, I made a few contacts with a desire to understand why she wouldn't take the job. I later found out from her acquaintances that she did not take the job because, first, I was from a different group than hers regardless of the offer made, and, second, the number of Hutus working in the organization was not to her comfort level. The main problem was that of security, discomfort and sense of guilt by association.

As Hutus dealt with guilt (of participation or association) over the murders, the Tutsis dealt with their own distrust of the Hutu community. Tutsis have been distrustful of the Hutus, and rightly so. In their hurt and grief over lost loved ones, some survivors of the genocide have felt a great lack of justice and observed the failure of the international community to support and contribute to the implementation of the promised international tribunal. Some have even seen people in the streets of Kigali who were heavily involved in the genocide. Some have been arrested, while evidence is lacking to arrest the others. It is important that the government continue to be as careful as they have been in arresting accused individuals. Without the measures the government has taken, including that of requiring evidence, people can easily get others into trouble for reasons known to them alone. It is important to protect people and strive for unity in the nation, but without true justice there can't be sincere unity. Under the previous government, killings and other social injustices went unchallenged. A part of what has contributed to the problems in Rwanda is a lack of a systemic justice that takes into account the social structure and context of the country.

More recently, sporadic ex-government-soldier attacks on the Zaire borders have combined with insurgencies in and around the capital city, causing uneasiness among both Tutsis and Hutus. The attacks have also raised the level of suspicion among people, seeming to add a little weight to the distrust of Hutus by the Tutsis. Though the RPF is a well-trained army with self-confidence, the ex-government soldiers create a worrisome environment for the present government and population as a whole. The exiled ex-government continues to enjoy strong support from the Zaire government and, to a certain extent, the French government. Some of the Hutus who were invited by the RPF to participate in the broad-based government forsook their responsibilities and decided to leave the country, to be involved in activities whose purpose is to disturb and sabotage the reconstruction of the country.

FOURTEEN

Tested and Proved

THE MOST TOUCHING stories in the Christian community are testimonies of individuals whose identity did not hinge on 'Hutu' or 'Tutsi', but who stood firm for their faith and sought to identify themselves with brothers and sisters in Christ. Many evil acts have been aired and televised. Unfortunately, stories of what I have decided to call 'the heroes of faith' have not been told. Quite often, such stories do not make news, and yet demonstrate the type of love and unity not only desired, but actually lived by many.

Despite the killings, the propaganda and the foreseeable consequences of associating with the Tutsis, there are individuals who took stands and accepted to pay whatever price was necessary instead of disowning and leaving their brothers and sisters to be unjustly killed. Testimonies have been shared on behalf of individuals who saved lives. In defiance of the savage atrocities against the Tutsis by the majority Hutu in Rwanda, exceptional cases have been reported in which certain 'born again' Christians demonstrated the contrary, thus testifying to the nature of God's children.

For example, a group of Hutu Christians blended with Tutsis in Gitarama prefecture were praying together when suddenly '*Interahamwe*' appeared, armed to kill. The militia asked the Hutus to separate themselves from the Tutsis, but they refused. The Gitarama gathering claimed they were all brothers and sisters in Christ. When the militia realized their request would be ignored, they killed them all save for one Hutu, who escaped the massacre and is the witness to this testimony.

A certain Habakurema Japhet, an elder in the Seventh Day Adventist Church, saved one Judith Uwingabilre, who had been thrown in a pit-latrine with her whole family. Judith was half dead when she was rescued from the pit. Unfortunately, the killing was still going on, and the poor man did not know what to do with the lady except to take her and hide her in the bush. Later he transferred her to another Hutu's family, where she received special assistance. The elder's sons also saved two brothers, Ndayisaba and Ndayambaje, and then escorted the pair to the Rwanda–Burundi border.[1]

A story has also been told of a church leader in the southern part of

Rwanda who hid a Christian man, then active in ministry. The church leader hid the man in the trunk of his car and managed to make it through many roadblocks guarded by militia. Unfortunately somewhere, somehow, this man had a change of heart. Before I heard his story, I had been disappointed by what he had to say to me while in my office in Nairobi. The man clearly expressed his view that Tutsi and Hutus will never live together in peace. He questioned if the Tutsis would not be able to take revenge. He wanted to know how any Hutu could live peacefully with people who had lost relatives to Hutu murderers. He blamed the killing of Hutu moderates and genocide of Tutsis on the RPF. To him, the murderers were defending themselves and therefore did what anybody else in their situation would have done. All this said, yet he saved a Tutsi life.

Another story similar to these is told of a Christian member of the Pentecostal Church who did not want to be identified. He had kept twenty-five people in his house during the killings.

Rwandan people have always saved each other's lives despite the political problems, massacres and bad leadership models the country has experienced. In the 1959 massacres, certain Tutsis' lives were saved by Hutus who had not been beguiled by politicians. Some Tutsis fled and left their cows and household belongings to Hutu friends, who proved to be faithful and kept them long into that extended exile. A case in point is my father's relationship with a Hutu friend of his, who also was a godfather to me. This man was my father's childhood friend. They were schoolmates who finished their school programme at the same time and then taught at the same school in the village of my birth. Throughout their single years they were friends. They both got married at about the same time. When the 1959 killings broke out, my father entrusted his cows to this man and fled the country. For years my father never heard from his friend. Later, my father came to learn that his friend had kept quiet to avoid putting his life in danger, as those in the country with relationships outside (especially among refugees) were considered friends of the enemies. Being labelled or accused of such a relationship had its own cost in the Rwandan politicized Hutu community, and was therefore a risky business. In the 1970s – over 10 years later – my father heard from his friend, who sent him money from one of his cows. From that time forward, their relationship was renewed until the death of my father in 1990s.

In the 1980s, I had my own personal experience with Rwandan Hutus who lived in Rwanda while I lived as a refugee outside Rwanda. I had no knowledge of the country except what I had learned from my parents, literature and news media. My contacts with Hutus from Rwanda, in Burundi where I lived, were minimal, and couched in suspicion. I always wondered what they thought about me being a Tutsi and never felt I could trust them. I felt we had nothing in common except being Rwandan, but also considered myself a Rwandan refugee rather than just a Rwandan.

While I was working in Kinshasa, Zaire, as a staff trainer with Campus Crusade, two Hutu couples from Rwanda joined our centre. Trainees and trainers at the centre lived on the same compound. I was not comfortable in that setting; later on I learned that they were not, either. Being uncomfortable on their part came from the feeling of being guilty by association: the Hutus had massacred Tutsis in 1959, 1961 and 1973. I was uncomfortable because I did not know if I could trust them. I seriously prayed for God to work in my life, and he did, as he did in theirs. One evening, I sat with one of the couples and we talked a lot about Hutu–Tutsi relationships in the Rwandan context. After sharp arguments and discussions that kept us from talking to each other for a few days, we came together in prayer and committed to understanding each other, and loving one another in Christ's love. These were remarkable relationships. Both couples and their families became my close friends. They became people I could counsel with and trust with personal matters. Throughout the period we were together at the centre in Zaire, they became the closest friends I had ever had. In 1982, when I was in Burundi as a national director of Campus Crusade, and my Hutu friends were in Rwanda, one of these friends came to visit me in Burundi. He and I had met time and again in Campus Crusade meetings and talked about visiting each other, but we would conclude our friendly discussions with 'Hey, I don't want your people to kill me!' We were joking, but the expression also reflected how uncomfortable we felt about each other's community. His visit and thoughtfulness marked my life and my friends' lives in Bujumbura, Burundi. Our friendship continued even though I left Africa for an extended period of time.

As I mentioned earlier, I visited Rwanda in 1993. These were difficult times to visit Kigali and most parts of the country. While in Kigali, I wanted to see my friend and his family, but I also was afraid of putting myself in danger and letting many people know I was in the country. These were times when the Rwandan government looked upon Tutsis outside Rwanda as '*Inkotanyi*', or members of the RPF. But because of the trust and the relationship we had built (though we had not been in touch for over 11 years), I called his house and found his wife. She and their children visited me at my hotel. Within days, her husband and I met and renewed our relationship. Our conversations and discussion surrounded the political environment of that time, and given the signing of the Arusha Accord we all thought that we would see each other again soon. Unfortunately, the killing broke out, and my friend and his family fled to Zaire. Shortly after that they were in Nairobi where I lived, and they knocked at my door. I welcomed them in after much hesitation and prayer. I did not know what role, if any, they had played in the mass killing of Hutu moderates and genocide of the Tutsis. But after much reflection I said to myself, 'If there is any time to show Christian love, and live according to God's great commandment, this is the time.' I had no other option but to stand by my Christian convictions as an ordained minister, pastor of both Tutsis and Hutus, let alone that my friend and his family of five had been good friends of mine. They stayed with us for a good two months until they were able to find a place of their own. Before the couple and their children, another couple and their two children had stayed with us. Unfortunately, that relationship later soured to the point where the man looked at my family and me as did most of his friends: not as Christian friends, but as RPF agents capable of getting them killed.

As there are stories of Hutus who tried to save lives, there are Hutu refugees who found refuge in Tutsi homes outside Rwanda. Tutsi families took food, distributed clothing and attended to the emergency needs of Hutu refugees. Except where politicians have used the situation to benefit themselves, Hutus and Tutsi have related well outside their own country. The RPF soldiers on the frontlines had as their objective to stop genocide and moved to save the lives of whoever they found in the bushes, vacated towns, villages and roadsides. There are stories of RPF soldiers who were killed by people they sought to protect.

Left alone by politicians and other power-seeking individuals, average people in the villages of Rwanda are able to live together. I believe that in the slow recovery of Rwanda, it is people like these tested and proved individuals who will model the kind of community living that Rwanda needs. I have seen people pointing out the heroes of faith, too. This finger-pointing is distinct from that of the betrayers whose intentions were to see lives ended: this pointing of a finger gives positive recognition of a person's love for humanity, their integrity and their love and caring. It is true that the genocide left people with scars and insurmountable problems, but when testimonies of the 'heroes of faith' spread and survivors acknowledge publicly those who rescued them, healing will take place.

Precolonial Rwandan people always lived together, sharing the good and the bad in their communities peacefully until some with selfish ambitions and goals moved into communities and started sowing seeds of division. Quite often, average people in the community have no serious problem with each other beyond normal community interpersonal problems. Every society has its own social problems, but it has been the experience in Rwanda (and elsewhere) that power politicians do nothing but take advantage of other people to fulfil their agendas.

The stories mentioned above are largely from the Christian community. I have to admit that in my learning about these things, I have had to depend very much on the stories told by people I trust and know. The people who saved lives are people who were willing to risk their own lives for their relatives, friends, neighbours or fellow believers. Hiding a Tutsi was considered hiding an enemy, and also a lack of Hutu solidarity. These people who stood firm at great risk to themselves are true heroes.

FIFTEEN

The Key of Confession

THE REPUTATION OF the worldwide Christian community has been hurt by the Rwandan church leaders' behaviour prior to and during the genocide. Even though there were indications of certain church leaders' desire to help in the process of peace negotiation and to strive for the unity of the Rwandan people, the Church as an institution failed in Rwanda. The Church was divided over the issue of ethnicity and the social injustices that have characterized Rwanda since the first Christian missionaries entered Rwanda. The ethnic conflict that found refuge in the young Church and continued to be nurtured by Rwanda's top church leaders contributed to the loss of the Church's credibility and caring spirit.

Throughout the 1994 killings, Christians around the world (and more specifically those concerned by the Rwandan situation) were wondering what role the Church could have in rebuilding the country, given the church leaders' position during the genocide. Non-Christians wondered if the Church would ever open its doors to the public again. Many non-Christians watching and listening to the situation on televisions and radios were shocked. They questioned the Christians' claim of faith, and many used their doubt in the Christians' sincerity to justify their own non-Christian attitudes and behaviour. There were Christians who thought that in order for the Church to resume a ministry that would have an impact in the lives of people, churchwide confession and the election of new leaders were essential.

Some Rwandans who follow that line of thinking are actually working hard on one aspect: the election of new leaders. With less emphasis on confession, they are finding genuine renewal hard to achieve because of an unrepentant spirit in the Church, and an election process that seems to be a power struggle rather than a spiritual concern of church life. Those who have managed to make changes in leadership have changed the top level, but not necessarily the people's thinking about the Rwandan ethnic conflict. A sincere church confession and change of heart for most church people is yet to come. The Church and church leadership need to rise above ethnic conflict, and church leadership conflict based on ethnic lines, to unity in Christ. The situation as it was during the war contributed to non-Christians' denial of their need to receive Christ. The behaviour of most church members, including their leaders, was outwardly no different from the non-Christians' conduct and therefore lacked the Christian testimony that would have made a significant difference.

The war situation in Rwanda and the Church's comportment challenged me personally to rethink Romans 12. The particular exhortation that Paul gives in his chapter can be summarized in three Christian duties: our duty to God, our duty to ourselves and our duty to our neighbours. What struck me in the Rwanda situation was the Christian conformity to evil acts. The devil definitely managed to blind certain church leaders, and to mislead a great majority of the church members. I believe that most Christians in Rwanda had heard the biblical teaching that calls followers of Jesus Christ to be non-conformists to this world. The scriptural challenge to Christians is to resist fashioning themselves according to worldly men, and certainly not to follow the multitude to do evil. Instead, if enticed by non-Christians, Christians are not to consent to them but rather take an opportunity to witness to them. Those I called 'the heroes of faith' in the Rwandan genocide did just that. As McCullum wrote in his book *The Angels Have Left Us*, they 'risked and often lost their lives to protect and minister to their people'.[1]

To the surprise of many people in Rwanda, including some Christians, church services resumed immediately following the RPF's takeover of the country, certain churches being packed to their maximum capacity. Initially, most people found in the capital city of Rwanda were new faces to Kigali. Faces in most churches were also new, then, with few old church members, and among new faces in the churches were old Rwandan refugees. In some churches, the initial church service organizers were from among the returnees who targeted the denominations they were connected with in countries of exile. The new organizers were either elders and ordained pastors in refugee resettlements where they lived, or church pastors in the national churches of their countries of asylum. Returning into the homeland, some had actually been eyeing the takeover of local church leadership situations as they thought that most of the former leaders would not want to return to Rwanda due to accusations of involvement in the genocide and compliance with the whole killing situation.

The church experience immediately after the genocide stopped was characterized by memorial services for genocide victims, survivors recognizing God's protection, and praise and thanksgiving for the end of the killing and for the homecoming of the refugees. As time went by, sermons on reconciliation and justice were heard in most churches around the country. As people moved quietly through the church services, with fresh memories of the mass killing and genocide around them, sad faces were observed and a sense of spiritual crisis and burden felt.

As people congregated in front of churches hugging and shaking hands as is the custom of greeting, there was also some finger-pointing, whispering and looks of suspicion. People lingered around to comfort one another, to share stories about the genocide and the loss of family members, and to talk about the adjustment required in the post-war environment. Communication was observed more among people who knew each other; others carefully chose to whom they introduced themselves. While many wanted to talk and make new friends, there were also those who seemed to be lonely and slowly withdrew from the crowds of people to head wherever they resided. In most cases, these were people with some kind of connection among the thousands who had just fled the country into Burundi, Tanzania and Zaire. Whatever their connections might have been, many were simply uncomfortable and somehow felt guilt.

After-church discussions throughout the world commonly centre on sermons and the people who delivered them. Former church leaders were also discussed after Rwandan services, and blamed for their roles in the genocide or their silence and therefore compliance with the situation. The discussions, especially of those concerned with church leadership, also involved enquiries into what should happen with former church leaders. Reorganization of church leadership is longed for across the country, but churches that have reorganized are facing church politics stirred up by former church leaders now in exile, or by other self-serving individuals in the church.

As churches resumed their responsibility (in most cases with new services and church activity organizers) the newly established government did not waste time in calling upon recent refugees to return home and participate in the rebuilding of the country. The call to return went hand in hand with an assurance of bringing justice to the murderers and planners of the genocide. Those with no direct involvement in the slaughter had nothing to fear and therefore had no reason to live in exile, but were being called home. The government knew that there were many innocent people who followed the killers into exile believing that the RPF would exact revenge for murdered Tutsis immediately after it reclaimed the country. Disregarding their fears, thousands heard the new government's plea and returned to their home country, and among the returnees came a few former church leaders and pastors to reclaim their church positions. Some of those positions were still vacant, others had been temporarily filled by either returnees or survivors of the genocide. Church leaders who stayed as refugees in exile continued to claim leadership responsibilities, thus trying to keep their positions vacant until they felt safe to return to Rwanda. There are even those who still want to appoint temporary 'acting leaders' on their behalf while remaining in residence outside the country, where some continue to be leaders of what they call 'the church in exile'.

Such situations have created church leadership crises based on power struggles and along ethnic lines. Where former leaders such as bishops, pastors and archbishops have returned, leadership crises have also mounted, with church members and pastors demanding that those with any association or involvement in the genocide be deposed from church leadership and replaced with new elected leaders. There is also a demand for the church to reorganize to integrate Tutsis into the leadership of the church in order to bring a new balance to the church leadership that was historically selected on the basis of ethnic origin or political motivations. The Church in Rwanda faces a serious structural and spiritual challenge that calls for a Christ-centred leadership.

The situation of former church leaders' involvement in and compliance with the genocide; the absence of key church leaders and a lack of official replacements; and the effect of extremist Hutu politics among the refugees in Burundi, Kenya, Tanzania and Zaire continue to contribute to the division of the church and to an unrepentant spirit in the Church. Certain denominations have somehow managed to 'keep a lid' on their internal conflicts, while others have engaged in public disputes that are often reflective of a power struggle. The longer it takes to find a church leadership solution, the more the tension tends to be viewed and interpreted from an ethnic perspective.

Some Christians, sick of the fighting in the Church, tired of politicking and individual kingdom-building, have moved out of the fighting churches to create small fellowships of believers that study Scripture, worship and pray for healing and forgiveness in the nation. These small fellowships have managed to attract people across denominational barriers and ethnic lines. At the same time, the returning Christian refugees of 1959 and their families are finding that they can't fit into the existing churches and the leadership conflicts that characterize them. They are moving to form fellowships and new churches that reflect the backgrounds of their churches in exile. It is not unusual to find Rwandan people who were in the same country of exile worshipping together and thus forming a church that reflects their country of exile.

The church leadership conflict situation in Rwanda is becoming more and more worrisome. I am personally concerned by the lack of confession and the subsequent self-serving attitude that I observe among Rwandan Christian leaders. Sometimes those who are calling for leadership changes are no different from the former leaders in that they don't seek God's leading for ministry, but have different motives. As one friend commented, a great number of people are moving into the Church or Christian ministry because of access to foreign money in the Church. The Church also remains a place for politics; hatred instead of love, disunity instead of unity, fights instead of conflict-resolution, politicizing instead of preaching a biblical message continue to find room in the Rwandan church. The politicizing of the Church, the divisions along ethnic lines, a church leadership orientation that favours one ethnic group, and a self-serving church leadership are not new phenomena in Rwanda. The Church needs to come to its senses, remember its role, and become the salt and light that it is called to be in its community.

Rwandan church leaders, both Catholic and Protestant, need to be reminded of the cross. Church leaders of the past have acted more like politicians and have in fact been better politicians than church leaders. Much of the tragedy that is being reaped is easily traced to the church leaders and not to politicians alone. The Church has contributed significantly to Rwandan conflicts as well as to the country's development. From the days of colonial missionaries, church leaders have spoken smoothly from both sides of their mouths. The paradoxical position of the Catholic Church in matters of politics, and the Protestant church leaders' support of the Habyarimana regime, cannot be denied. The Church has been contaminated through the lack of spiritual leadership. Even a casual observer of Rwandan church history would note that politicking in the Church has gone from bad to worse, and usually unchallenged. A Christ-centred ministry has been given little consideration by traditional power-brokers in the Rwandan church. A friend making comments about Rwandan church leaders after the events of 1994 said, 'For us, church leaders have replaced Jesus Christ! As his servants, his representatives and ambassadors, they have been commissioned to carry on with his work, and we trust and believe every word they say.'

In a sense my friend is right: church leaders have much influence, especially in societies such as Rwanda. The sad part is that the leaders have not been good models of Christian living. Many church leaders and church members in Rwanda have surrendered their minds not to the things of God, but to the advantages of co-opting colonialism and political concerns for their benefit. Ethnic divisions and materialism have invaded the thinking of church leaders to the degree that their 'salt' has been diluted.

To have a significant ministry to the Rwandan population, the Church must be reconciled, with God and among fellow Christians: there has to be a radical change in the conduct of church leaders and members alike. The Church is called to be different from the world, but the tendency has been to be like the world, and the genocide shed some light on that conduct. Rwandan political development since the arrival of colonialism and Christian missions has sucked the Church in like a sponge, and the Church's conformity has been visible since that time. Hopefully, the new Kigali government will keep its hands clean in the matters of the Church, just as they have so far. My prayer is that the Church can divorce itself from the kind of church–state relationships that seek favours from politicians in exchange for the Church's prophetic voice. The former Vice President of Kenya, Mr Mwai Kibaki, put it well while addressing members of the National Council of Churches of Kenya: 'The church leaders should not spend their time praising politicians; we have enough people to praise us. Your task is to correct us when we go wrong and need to be reminded of the justice of God, and to pray for us.'[2] Respect for church leaders does not come from their association with political leaders, but from their relationship with God, a relationship proven in non-conformity to ungodly things. Christian leaders are often caught in the political trap of their countries; this has been the case for Rwandan church leaders. David Gitari in his book *Let the Bishop Speak* wrote:

> A position of active and positive support for the state is obviously the easiest position for the Church to adopt; however, it is also the most unfortunate posture in which the Church can be found. Churches which are favored by the state find it very tempting to respond by giving full support to their patron; but they tend to suffer most when the regime they support is removed and replaced by a new government.[3]

It is likely that Bishop Gitari was well aware of the Rwandan situation; at least his insight describes exactly where the Rwandan church leadership has been.

It is important that the Church go back in history, check how it has failed the Rwandan society, and confess. Church leaders have to accept their responsibility, come to the Lord with a truly repentant spirit and be reconciled with God. In the past, the Church never addressed the issue of ethnicity. The avoidance of the issue has, in a sense, created ethnic group solidarity among the people who were threatened by the politics of both the Church and the previous government. The political threat, both international and internal, caused both the Rwandan Church and the previous government to create an environment that shaped church members' lives. Now that the climate is one of openness, they seem to be free to address the issue of a church leadership that was based on ethnicity; but Christians often avoid conflicting issues for fear of being considered less than Christian. The Church has to be willing to model openness and participation in leadership matters for differences to be resolved. This can't happen, however, if today's Rwandan church and church leaders will not come before the Lord and confess.

Confession is the key to resolving the conflict in the Rwandan church. The Church will not have a significant role in reconciling the people of Rwanda if it is not reconciled to God. As far as church leadership is concerned, there has to be a win–win structure, based on godliness and demonstrable characteristics of church leadership, in candidates. Rwandan ecclesiastical and government policies seem to have been developed and perpetuated on the 'win–lose' model of leadership: it is time that Rwandans learned the difference.

The newly established government has set an example that needs to be followed and even improved upon to set Christian leadership standards. It is sad to see the Church having to select its leadership based on ethnic and political factors, rather than the biblical qualities of a leader. The church leaders have to remember that they are behavioural models for the Church and often for the community around them. In 1 Peter 5.2 the Scripture underscores the necessity of modelling through leadership:

> To the elders among you, I appeal as a fellow elder, a witness of Christ's suffering and one who also will share in the glory to be revealed: be shepherds of God's flock that is under your care, servicing as overseers – not because you must, but because you are willing, as God wants you to be; not greedy for money, but eager to serve; not lording it over those entrusted to you, but being examples to the flock.

While I was travelling in Ethiopia, a church leader approached me and said that he had been praying for Rwanda. For him, until the church leaders can repent before the Lord and seek his face, there will be no peace in Rwanda. Given the role of the Church and its past contribution to the political development of the country, I agree with him. As the Church contributed to the conflict in Rwanda, the Church can also significantly contribute to the biblical reconciliation of Rwandan people. But first it must be reconciled to God through confession.

Part Six

—

Reconciliation, Rehabilitation – and Demolition

SIXTEEN

Laying the Foundation for Reconciliation

BY EARLY 1995, reconciliation was the hot topic for non-government organizations (NGOs), church- and non-church-related alike. Church-related agencies started their reconciliation strategies from outside the country, most of these organizations being based in Nairobi, Kenya, with branches in places like Goma, Zaire, and Ngara, Tanzania.

The aim of these organizations was to adopt a strategic reconciliation ministry that was focused on both refugees outside the country and the home population. The target groups to be reconciled were the Tutsis and the Hutus. First, reconciliation meetings and preparatory workshops were held in Nairobi to discuss what needed to be done and to lay the groundwork. Rwandan populations from student communities and Christian organizations were invited by concerned agencies to discuss ways of addressing the reconciliation issue. Unfortunately, those first contacted and invited to the initial meetings were Hutu students from some of the theological institutions. According to Karl Dortzbach, the Hutu students made the move, approaching his organization for healing and reconciliation workshops for Hutu and Tutsi refugees.[1] The fact is that Tutsi students, though not many, were initially not informed and therefore absent from these foundational meetings. Their absence gave rise to some shaky first impressions of the reconciliation programme throughout the Rwandan Tutsi community in Nairobi. The organizations coordinating the reconciliation effort continued their discussion with a monoethnic group associated with the ethnic group that was spearheading genocide in Rwanda. Members of the Hutu student group visited refugee camps in Tanzania and came back to Nairobi with interesting and varied findings. Some were convinced that reconciliation between Tutsis and Hutus was almost impossible, but since there were organizations with money to be spent, they saw no reason why they could not spend that money on themselves and on other unrelated individual or refugee concerns. I remember one coming into my office then in Nairobi, and proudly stating that he could not help but 'eat the dollar'.

The reconciliation effort persisted. Organizations positioned themselves in neutral settings where they thought they could easily manage to get Rwandan Christians from inside Rwanda, and Rwandan refugees in Zaire and Tanzania, together for reconciliation meetings and workshops. Some organizations went as far as drawing maps that showed areas where strategic reconciliation teams would be based in order to reach the Rwandan population in the four corners of the country, while also targeting people in the camps outside. Experts in reconciliation ministries, with experience in Liberia and other African countries with ethnic conflicts, were brought in. Many were stationed in Nairobi, Kenya; others set up in the areas of Goma and Bukavu, Zaire, and still others in Ngara, Tanzania.

Organizations with reconciliation ministry goals started thinking about reconciliation and setting their goals and objectives long before the genocide was stopped. While most organizations pushing for reconciliation were outside the country, inside Rwanda, church agencies and other organizations pushed for reconciliation programmes while the government called for justice.

In my opinion, it was too soon to call for reconciliation. If anything was needed, it was healing for the survivors and trauma counselling for both survivors and refugees in the camps. It was the killers that got the world's attention and not the survivors. I believe that many, and myself included, did not know how to relate to the genocide survivors. More than that, most of those who called for reconciliation were forming reconciliation groups using and training reconciliation facilitators from one ethnic group. Agencies were so sold on reconciliation that some were using emergency relief supplies to manipulate the process and force the issue. Some funding organizations were not willing to fund programmes that did not include reconciliation plans. While 'reconciliation' was becoming a favourite word among NGOs and a money-making project for good proposal writers, it was becoming a painful word and insult for genocide survivors and Tutsis in general. People in the country, especially those who were mourning their loved ones and relatives, wanted to hear and see justice.

Church seminars and mission crusades have been organized by both Rwandan insiders and people from the outside. Evangelistic organizations and other non-profit Christian organizations rushed to develop and present strategies of reconciliation to the Rwandan church. What has been the response?

The response is varied. Most Rwandans, especially non-Christians, might contend that there have been no visible results. Christians, on the other hand, might respond according to their church background and present church experience. Christians attending churches with deep divisions, fights and power struggles for leadership will understandably be negative about the results of reconciliation efforts. In fact, they see no way out until there is a true and radical change in the church leaders' behaviour, including a sincere commitment to the Lord in faith and deed. On a positive note, individual Christians involved in small groups without a centralized leadership based on denomination can often recount positive reconciliation experiences.

Reconciliation programmes are good and wonderful! However, they have not offered the foundation upon which Rwandans can rebuild their country. 'Reconciliation' is a very political word with deep political connotations, not only in Rwanda, but in many parts of the world. Reconciliation as presently done and discussed in Rwanda will not, I am afraid, produce lasting results and therefore will have but limited impact. Most workshops have addressed the issues through wonderful speakers, facilitators and small-group leaders. The process, however, has been technical and mechanical. The cultural context and the context of the crisis are often misunderstood by the organizers of workshops and seminars. The in-house church reconciliation programmes have been affected by lack of church leaders' repentance. The general distrust that still lingers between the groups affects the interpersonal relationships and the community's interaction, therefore making it hard to see the result that many have been looking for. The lack of visible results also contributes to some people's downplaying the need for reconciliation, who feel that justice has not been done. These are people who are still in great pain and grief. The other thing that needs to be understood is the level of trauma for those who were in the country, and even for those who came from outside and saw the atrocities. Healing is definitely going to take time. Therefore the process demands patience, but people are often impatient.

Genocide scars are going to be difficult to heal, given the reminders that are everywhere in the Rwandan community. Travelling around the country, you meet orphans and widows who are victims of the 1994 carnage. The stories they tell, the memories they have, the fears, the renewed violence in certain parts of the country, the rising anger and mistrust – all these make it hard for any type of reconciliation to take place. Individual reconciliation based on the biblical process of reconciliation can still happen despite the insurgencies and general mistrust in the country. For the Church as a whole, the continued working relationships and collaboration of Hutu church leaders with the exiled church leaders cause suspicion and raise questions, especially when vacant church positions can't be filled because of the influence of exiled church leaders. The same type of influence creates interpersonal issues and questions that can be solved only through dialogue in a proper climate.

Since July 1994, the new Rwandan government has done a number of things with limited funds, human resources and infrastructure. And they have accomplished much to lay the groundwork for reconciliation. The new government has shown a desire for, and commitment to, change that is focused on bringing the Rwandan community to unity and peace. Whether political developments and socioeconomic realities will discourage the government's efforts to reunify the Rwandan population and continue the repatriation of refugees, no one can tell yet. The truth of the matter is that, given the circumstances, the government has been doing as much as they can to bring an atmosphere of reconciliation to a terribly wounded country. From the very beginning of the new government, its leaders have tirelessly worked to organize inclusive social events like cultural festivals, sport competitions and youth activities; the government has campaigned for peace and reunification. But all these could come to nothing if they are not taken to heart by individuals who feel that justice is yet to come. Though arrests of suspected murderers have been made, there are others still openly moving around in the cities and villages of the country. Where survivors and witnesses of the genocide have not been kidnapped and killed, they are intimidated. As African Rights reported, 'Two years on, the genocide extremists remain active, hunting down and murdering the survivors of the genocide, and also targeting Hutu witnesses to intimidate them into silence and, if necessary, kill them too.'[2]

The scars of the genocide are still fresh. Rwanda's capital city and large towns may look freshly painted, with bullet holes filled and ruins cleaned up, but however far along the physical repairs may be, genocide is a live reality among Rwandans. Though the government has done a marvellous job and continues to do what they can in their financially difficult situation, they would like to bring justice to bear to a greater degree. The move to reconciliation has indeed been premature for those affected, and yet there is a real need for some kind of reconciliation programme after a situation like Rwanda's. The reminders are just too many and too great for people to bear, and all the more if justice is not done to help alleviate people's heavy hearts. A lack of justice will only contribute to another slaughter, and the Rwandan population will remain greatly divided and paralysed by fear and distrust of each other. This is why the government's priority is to punish killers as a prerequisite to reconciliation. The international community has to understand that failure to start and accelerate the international tribunal process is nurturing a serious problem. The hundreds of prisoners lingering in Rwandan jails as they await trial contribute to the public fear of being arrested.

For many years, the Rwandan church (and Christians as a whole) have avoided talking about ethnic tensions and differences in the Church and country. Yet acts of discrimination found a ready home in the Church and among church leaders. The situation as it is provides an opportunity for the Church in Rwanda to lay a proper foundation for Christians to live together.

The proper foundation for the Christian Church is Jesus Christ, who taught the necessity of laying a solid foundation. Rwandan Christians have heard, I am sure, the biblical truth that 'Unless the Lord builds the house, its builders labour in vain' (Psalm 127.1). Genuine reconciliation is characterized first by reconciliation with God. Unless the hearts of men and women in Rwanda are changed by God's love through Christ, Christians in Rwanda will be hard pressed to contribute to the building of their nation. It is time now for the Church to dialogue honestly about the issue that has destroyed the country. The Church cannot afford to keep quiet any more. Church programmes are needed to get people involved in activities that provide the opportunity for them to be busy together. As Rwandans know, there have been many words and promises. It is now time for real action that demonstrates love and unity. Sermons have been too many and too unproductive regarding the issues of unity, love and real reconciliation. Christians should learn to lay the foundation of conflict-resolution based on biblical principles of forgiveness. It is almost as though when the majority of Rwandans talk about reconciliation they forget about asking forgiveness, and so forget that sin can still result in unhappy consequences. The real foundation of Christianity results from together breaking open the Scripture, and letting the Holy Spirit of God work in the hearts of those concerned. It is seeking God's will and God's leading from his Word.

Rwandans who are serious about reconciliation in biblical terms have first to acknowledge the real issue. But Rwandan Christians especially have avoided talking about the real issue. It is as if to admit one's failure to love another person because of ethnic distinction makes one less of a Christian. Christians have to be honest with themselves. Clearly, negativity about reconciliation, and assumptions about its impossibility among Rwandans, have to stop if reconciliation is to be realized. The method sometimes renders it ineffective. The quality of human relationships in the Church, or in the community as a whole, affects the degree of reconciliation within it. There is no question that ethnic hatred could be avoided in the Church if church leaders were to reflect relationship-building based on sincere Christian beliefs. Most Rwandans try to avoid history when faced with their ethnic interpersonal relationship problems. They do not allow time to work on them. The best methodology the Church can encourage is dialogue. It is important that the Church try not to avoid, but rather to acknowledge, her failure and confront ethnic hatred rather than frighten parties on both sides of the line.

So I am not saying that reconciliation is impossible. I believe reconciliation is possible, but only in the right environment and cultural context, and accompanied by justice. I do believe that reconciliation from a Christian perspective is understood differently than from a secular political perspective, but justice is a critical element in both. Reconciliation without justice is not reconciliation.

There is no question that reconciliation, trauma counselling, and any teaching on healing and forgiveness are best done through dialogue and interaction in small groups. The one-to-one type of programme to unify people and help solve their conflict is not possible, given the realities of Rwanda; but certain things can be done to help create an environment conducive to reconciliation and healing: bringing justice and providing a secure environment in the country are two of them.

Church people should be the first to understand that Rwandans have to live together. Where will one group go if both groups can't live together? It is impossible to eliminate a group of people completely. Instead of those in power trying to unify people, the past Rwandan leadership has always sought to divide people. 'Winners' and 'losers' should learn to live together in the Rwandan society. Church people have more in common than the rest of the population, and their cause is more powerful. There is no question but that they should take the lead in true reconciliation.

SEVENTEEN

Rehabilitation

WHILE I WAS SITTING in my Kigali office one day, a very young Japanese lady appeared with a little backpack and a camera in her hand. After a few minutes of self-introduction, she opened up her backpack to show me postcards her organization had made out of pictures they had taken in one of the Rwandan orphanages I was familiar with. She told me that her organization had raised some money for Rwanda, and according to her country's relief money policy it should be spent on the purpose for which it was raised. During the early stages of the establishment of NGOs in Kigali, two men from her organization had come for need-assessments, contacts and relationship-building. All that done, the organization still was not sure what they should do, but felt the need to do something. Unfortunately, they had no funds available to them at the time and wanted to go back and raise money needed for a community-type rehabilitation programme. They raised high hopes with a number of people, and returned to their country for fundraising. The young lady had come without money, but explored possibilities of where they could spend some of the funds they had raised. She said that her organization was under pressure to spend the money they had raised, and she was in my office to find a place for it. The organization had raised funds without a clear goal of what to do in Rwanda, and yet the needs in the country were staggering.

Representatives of a large US-based organization turned up unannounced with cameras and notepads, and pens in their pockets, hungry for genocide stories. Over a lunch conversation they told me that they could raise thousands of dollars to help in rehabilitation programmes. The main problem was that they did not want to set up an office and be operational in Rwanda, but rather find partners who would use the money they were in a position to raise. After a few days in the country, they left for home with enough stories and pictures to communicate the rehabilitation needs in the country. They were committed to come back with thousands of dollars, ready to find a capable partner to use the funds. As far as I know at the time of writing, they have not returned to Kigali.

While I was on home leave from the field where I worked, a group of people asked me about a ministry I had not heard of in Rwanda. Apparently, some of the people in the group had contributed funds designated to help orphans in the country. I simply communicated that I had not heard of such an organization. In my work and working relationships with other NGOs in Rwanda, and especially Christian NGOs, I had come across many, and thought I knew all the Western-based organizations. The one in question had raised a large sum of money for the purpose of benefiting Rwandan orphans; I promised the group that I would look into the situation and report back to them. It was not too long before I travelled back to Kigali, where I researched and found no such organization to be active in Rwanda. The organization continued its fundraising activities, I was told, and thousands of dollars have been contributed. The organization's leaders have also travelled back and forth in the country. A recent report I heard was that an update on the organization's work had been published to encourage donors to continue their contributions. At the same time, unhappy donors had contacted the Rwandan Embassy to express their concern over the organization.

Rwanda has been a bonanza for fundraisers around the world. The Rwandan genocide situation has been used by a number of organizations to boost their incomes with little (if any) contribution in return to the rehabilitation, reconciliation and relief of Rwanda. All that said, there were a great number of organizations that did contribute significantly and properly to the rebuilding of the country. One cannot help but mention an overwhelming presence of NGOs in Rwanda immediately following the RPF victory and takeover of the country. The presence of UN and relief agencies gave the impression of an over-supplied relief situation, and yet many of the relief resources were not reaching their proper destinations.

Rehabilitation was an undoubted need. The country had been virtually destroyed and was in obvious need of whatever monetary or material assistance could be allocated to genocide survivors, returning refugees and social services. Church leaders in Rwanda wasted no time in putting rehabilitation on their church- and nation-building agendas. Some church leaders and local Christian NGO leaders with contacts in the Western countries embarked on fundraising journeys. A casual observer might say the drives met with success, but fundraisers within Rwanda often demonstrate the level of success in their fundraising by the type of car they drive, the houses they live in and the kind of lifestyle they pursue.

The lack of accountability and integrity in some organizations has been reflected in the emergency relief operations, the distribution of goods, and then in the funds designated to rehabilitation. Rehabilitation has become a money-making concern for some. There are church leaders with experience in proposal-writing and with previous relationships with donor communities in European and other Western countries. Most of the bishops and other top church leaders with a 'mother church' in the West have either travelled for weeks at a time or made appearances for rehabilitation funds. The leaders now outside the country have done the same, with a major emphasis on assisting refugees in the camps of Zaire, Tanzania and Burundi. Funds have been given to such leaders as mentioned above in both cash and cheque form. The donors seem not to care about how the money is spent, though most of them indicate that they require written reports of how funds are used.

Former Rwandan church leaders now in Kenyan exile live like kings. They live in expensive homes, drive nice cars and dress well. Their lifestyles have not at all been affected by the fact that they now are refugees who lost much of what they owned. Instead, many of them live a more prosperous lifestyle than they did in the home country. The flock they supposedly lead live in difficult circumstances in the camps of Tanzania, Zaire and Burundi, while they live in the bungalows and nice apartments of Nairobi. Politicking characterizes the lives of some, and much of their time, funds and energy is spent in activities that are not necessarily church- or relief-related. Funds are also reported to have been used to disturb the peace and corrupt church members inside Rwanda in an effort to prevent elections of new church leaders that might replace them. They want to continue to lead from their base in exile.

The lack of accountability and integrity is not limited to those outside the country. A few church leaders inside Rwanda have also received thousands of dollars and used them in many different ways. Some funds have been used for relief, rehabilitation and continued assistance to the needy and suffering. But it is also true that funds given by evangelical churches, ecumenical churches and Christian organizations of the same nature have been used to widen divisions and to reinforce the invisible walls of hate.

The most visible problems of this type have been observed in the Episcopal Church of Rwanda. Judging by my telephone conversation and interview with one of the church priests, the church is in disgrace. Plans to fill vacant dioceses have failed, and serious church fights have erupted in church services in various locations on different occasions. Relief and rehabilitation funds have been diverted to hire youth fighters from marketplaces to come and drag pastors from church pulpits, disrupting services and even beating individuals who resist. These thugs have pulled a bishop out of his chair, have cleared sanctuaries filled with worshippers and have overturned tables with communion elements. Pick-up trucks purchased from Christian organizations with church-donated funds have been seen transporting these young fighters to wherever a certain 'self-imposed' bishop was to be. He is considered 'self-imposed' mainly because he considers himself the rightful heir of the diocese, while another group considers him not only the wrong person to lead the diocese, but also a murderer and participant in the genocide. The story in Kigali and among Christians is that he also uses funds available to him for corruption, and for power struggles. According to another interview (with a person not to be identified), this bishop accused of many wrongdoings during the Rwandan genocide is highly regarded by the Anglican community outside Rwanda. The bishop was the first among exiled Rwandan church leaders to return to Kigali immediately after the end of genocide, despite numerous accusations, while seven other bishops remained outside the country. While living in Rwanda, he has kept his family in exile and travels back and forth to see them. A lot of funds have been given to him by a number of organizations, for church relief activities, to reconstruct destroyed buildings and to resume church programmes and activities. Reports are that diocesan resources are used to run his personal affairs and business. He is not accountable to anybody as a bishop, except to the donor community, to which he provides written reports of his expenditures when required.

The issue of accountability in the Rwandan Protestant churches is not new. Even before the genocide, most Rwandan church leaders were known as authoritarian types. Most had enriched themselves from foreign church aid money and enjoyed a lifestyle that was far beyond the reach of most Rwandans, thereby alienating themselves from the people they served. Mercedes-Benz and Audis were not unusual cars for them to drive. Their houses were opulent, and their bank accounts secure, while most of their local pastors could not afford a bicycle. Disputes, such as those happening now over leadership positions, are motivated by the leaders' desire to serve themselves rather than to alleviate the church-created conflicts that shamed church members.

Rehabilitation money in the wrong hands is a serious problem that threatens the unity and peace of people in Rwanda. When the money comes from well-meaning Christian organizations and churches in the West and is misused by church leaders who are not accountable to their church congregations, the donor organizations are viewed as supporters and close collaborators of such leaders. Without knowing it, donor organizations contribute to the rebuilding of power struggles in churches, and to deeper divisions. Situations have been reported where money given for reconciliation programmes has rather been used for separatist political activities. Donor organizations with no requirement of accountability risk rebuilding the Church on false and rotten foundations that need to be destroyed.

It has often been said that in most relational cultures, business principles are based on who you know. This could be said for most cultures and countries, and more so in the Western-based donor countries. Donor Christian organizations tend to offer assistance in situations of relief through acquaintances, either missionaries or nationals. I once challenged an organization that was basically dumping their money irresponsibly just because they knew an influential person on the receiving end. The person receiving funds was involved in many different personal businesses as well as supporting rebel fighters aiming to overthrow his country's leadership. There was one individual in the organization who knew the church leader on the receiving end and defended him with all his power. Sadly, the relationship was so strong that he was not able to believe or to rationalize that the church leader was engaged in such acts. Whenever we sent auditors to the church to evaluate the leader's work and check the usage of funds, there was always a reason why the timing wouldn't work for the bishop. Several times, the donor's field auditors visited the church leader's office, were well-received in special official ceremonies and ended up leaving without doing their work. Others were bribed and brought false reports back to the donor base. Today, the church leader has been discovered. Although he still receives money from a number of donors, he is known for his actions and only those sharing his view of things give him money for his personal kingdom.

Rehabilitation is a wonderful project and needs to be encouraged, but there are times when it leads to perpetuating rather than solving a problem. Before work begins, a clear problem has to be defined, and the best way I find is to deal with rehabilitation situations from a problem-solving approach. One could ask whether there is an alternative to rehabilitation. My personal answer is yes, there is one, especially in situations of problems created by ethnic conflicts and therefore rife with social and interpersonal relationship problems.

But it is a radical alternative.

EIGHTEEN

Demolition

RATHER THAN REHABILITATION in Rwanda, perhaps demolition needs to be considered first. 'Rehabilitation' in the sense used in Rwanda today suggests and implies restoration. One gets the impression that most Rwandan former church leaders want to revive and restore much of what was going on, with no desire to go in a different direction. Visiting churches around the country and interaction with pastors often results in discussions about physical rebuilding needs. The danger of physical rehabilitation and the money involved, as has been the case, is of rebuilding on rotten and damaged foundations – not just physical in nature – that deserve to be demolished. Rehabilitation funds available to some church leaders are being used to manipulate people and buy votes. The money helps the corrupt leaders to regain their influence at the expense of unresolved conflicts. The invisible walls of hatred, church practices and decisions based on discrimination, and authoritarian as opposed to servant leadership, all have to be demolished.

Much of what shocked the world and the Christian community around the world was the silence and behaviour of the Christian church leaders in Rwanda. Given that what is known about church leadership in Rwanda at this point is negative, the Church in Rwanda should take advantage of the opportunity to find godly new leaders. Rwandan churches cannot afford to elect key church leaders on the same basis as before the genocide. Much of the politicking surrounding church leadership selection is re-forming, and the same old games characterized by church politics are being played; money has regained control of independent minds. Church leadership that is self-serving and manipulative in nature will not contribute to the building of the nation; rather, it will return the country to chaos.

Robert Coleman once stated, 'Leadership must be public in doing good if it is to gain confidence, trust . . . leadership which is public models for the congregation a style of being responsible and accountable to God and His people.'[1] Let us be frank: the Rwandan top church leaders' behaviour, values and commitment do not seem to reflect or to have reflected Christ-likeness. If Rwandan Christians imitated the models provided by their leaders, no wonder the Church lost credibility.

Church leadership principles need to be based on sound biblical theology and teaching in the Church. The Rwandan church leadership situation needs to be studied from an objective viewpoint that would allow for listening and observing the church situation. The Rwandan church is at present a mixture of returning refugees and survivors who remained within the country. There is a lot to learn, and especially in the context of the Rwandan ethnic conflict and recent genocide: a sound and prayerful analysis needs to be made, in order to avoid future pitfalls.

One of the major components in church leadership is the recognition and acknowledgement of Christ's role as the head of the Church. The church in Rwanda needs transformational leaders – Jesus was a transformational leader! Bernard Bass defined such leadership as 'a kind of motivation which increases the wakefulness of people about what they want'.[2] Though the former church leadership may not want change, there are people who do, for reasons no other than a desire to live a Christian life in harmony with their fellow Rwandans. Church leadership, the social environment and the Rwandan community need change that I believe the Church, with proper leadership, could help bring about. Leighton Ford wrote, 'Transformational leadership is . . . a double-edged sword. When we look for leaders who can transform, we need to be aware that people can be transformed down in destructive ways as well as up to lift their level of achievement.'[3] The destructive ways mentioned here spring forth when people follow leaders blindly without question, and blind obedience is one of the Rwandan church member's characteristics. Even in the 1994 genocide, I believe that there were people who followed whatever their leaders decided to do, without ever exercising their own minds. Previous church leadership criteria need to be forgotten, and completely removed from the present leadership. A church leader is a father who nurtures his children – I like the Catholic term 'father'. The negative potential of transformational leadership should not scare anybody away from making necessary changes, especially in the Rwandan situation. Given Rwandan church history, the potential problem of this double-edged sword needs much attention.

The comportment of Rwandan church members during the genocide situation raised a key issue in missions, that of Christian nurture. 'Nurture' is a term also used for care and feeding. In church life, it addresses the level of discipleship, church nurture, and the issue of conversion. The size of the reported Christian population in the country, and church members' involvement in the genocide (as has been discussed and reported), suggest some success in evangelism, but a profound lack of discipleship. We are aware that the well-known East African Revival, born at Gahini Parish of the Episcopal Church in Kibungo district, produced an amazing number of new believers in these countries, and fruits of the revival are still visible to a certain extent. What seems to have been lacking, and therefore an issue that raises concern for Christian growth in Rwanda, is the discipling of believers. Current emphasis has been very much on repentance, and new converts need to be discipled, or else there will be no lasting growth. Christian nurture seems to be the greatest need of the African church now, as more and more people (actually thousands every day) make a commitment for Christ. More and more, in one conference after another, the African church is realizing her greatest need is discipleship.

Fuller once remarked that 'many people are turning to Christ, but they are not being discipled. So, they are drifting into syncretism.'[4] Rwandan genocide survivors who tell stories of the killings often indicate syncretistic beliefs and practices performed by the killers to keep the spirits of their victims from bothering them at any time in the future. They also indicate that the killers would perform certain practices with the body parts of their victims. Curiously, some of these killers were church attenders. Missionaries and nationals who are concerned and have written on the dangers of syncretism seem to indicate that syncretistic tendencies flow from lack of discipleship. We must remember that the impetus of the Great Commission is to *make disciples*. An initial commitment to Jesus Christ is crucial, but it is an early step in fulfilling the Great Commission; the Church's task demands comprehensive discipleship.

The Rwanda situation underscores all we have discussed above. Rwanda is the home of the East African Revival, and of a population generally known as Christian. People still ask how what happened could have occurred in the context of a rich Christian background. The answer, I believe, lies in the lack of Christian nurture following conversion. Evangelistic messages have always been central to the preaching and teaching of Rwandan pastors and local evangelists. But what then?

The Lord Jesus Christ has commanded his Church to make disciples of every nation. Regardless of where one is, even in the present Rwandan context, every Christian is called upon to be a witness for Christ. The discipling and Christian nurturing of Rwandan Christians needs to change and take a new model: a model that addresses the Rwandan culture much better than the Western model of formal classroom learning.

It has been my emphasis in this book that Rwandan church leaders followed the model of church leadership provided to them by the early Rwandan church leaders. The Church–state relationship that was characterized by church leaders holding political positions is nothing new. In the Catholic Church, the political involvement of church leaders and representation on the Central Committee of the Rwandan government dates from the colonial days through the start of the most recent genocide. For the Protestant church, the involvement of nationals is recent; but when it started, it started at full speed, to make up for lost time. From colonial times to the 1960s, Protestant missionaries had tried to keep away from politics, even though they were associated with the Tutsis. The Tutsi association was the result of the missionaries coming out in the open and addressing discriminatory issues of the time, including the killings of 1959 and 1962.

A new model for Christian living and church leadership is needed. I have always believed and continue to believe that the Traditional African Education (TAE) or 'informal learning' model offers an excellent approach to Christian discipleship in Rwanda. Traditional African Education has been defined by Boateng as 'Africa's heritage in education'.[5] The term 'disciple' designates a learner, as in the sense of an apprentice. According to Kittel it implies a personal attachment of the learner to the master that shapes the disciple's whole life.[6] In the learning process of TAE, informal and non-formal methods of training or educating prevailed. Fafanuwa lists three pillars of educational process that are common to Africa and very much so for Rwanda, and these are: observation, imitation and participation.[7] The observation, imitation and participation model of training or informal education, when applied, can be very helpful and relevant to the Rwandan church and therefore to solving problems. Discipleship is a ministry to God, and therefore requires a biblical goal. Luke 6.40 tells us that the goal of discipleship is 'likeness', ultimately, the likeness of Christ.

The Rwandan church needs to become a worshipping church and move away from being a people-pleasing church that tends to stand alongside politicians and follow lines of ethnic conflict. This worship must be a true active response to God, where his worth is declared. The people need to come together in celebration of God. Godly men and women in the Rwandan churches need to rethink the role of the Church, and be willing to effect a radical change, a total demolition of the walls that have divided the society. The Church needs to be positioned for new ministry ideas and concepts that will involve all Rwandans without discrimination. New visions must engage the Church in participatory learning, and propose new models of leadership. A climate of healthy dialogue is critical for relationship-building, healing and forgiveness.

One of the most effective ways to help the Rwandan community, I believe, is to help demolish the invisible walls of guilt that block sincere communication, close relationships and the kind of dialogue that leads to peace and unity. As we have seen, guilt may have a corporate as well as an individual focus. To those who know God and profess to be Christians, guilt becomes a breach in their relationship with God and other people. To demolish guilt, one has to make right with God. Christians have to know that God is our deliverer from the bondage of guilt. Guilt comes from sin or association with sinful acts, and only God can break this bondage. Through Jesus Christ this has been done, but we still have to confess sin for what it is. Repentance in biblical terms means a change of heart. Rwandans need a change of heart in order not to rehabilitate their evildoing, or build on invisible walls that should be demolished. Church leaders and pastors in Rwanda can play a significant role in building and nurturing people who hold painful memories of genocide or guilt, once confession has taken place. Pastoral counselling can lead Rwandans into the realization of God's forgiveness.

Rwanda's is a relational culture. In such cultures, the Church can be an excellent agent of change. In previous chapters, I have mentioned the fact that hatred between the two major Rwandan groups was nurtured in the Church starting from colonial days, and with results. The same avenue could be used for positive change in Rwanda. The Church provides one of the best contexts for social interaction. Church ministries that have tended to divide people, or to discriminate with one group against the other, can be geared to clearing misunderstandings, discussing social issues and providing fresh opportunities for people to learn about each other. The Rwandan political society has successfully used the Church for its political agenda. Why can't Christians use the Church for Christian unity, love and community caring? Sometimes Christians are not aware of the power and influence of Christianity in their own community.

Without a genuine love, the Rwandan people will not hear what is said without distortion. It is for the Church to develop an atmosphere of loving relationships among Rwandans, a positive climate. This positive climate should also help people express their feelings when they are with each other. Without a healthy climate in the Church, people will not pull together and grow together. There will always be a polarization in the

Church and community. The Church can offer a message of hope to Rwandans, and challenge the fear people continue to live in.

The Church has to provide *all* Rwandans with a sense of belonging. Today, the Church needs to be a place for healing, witnessing and fellowship. I believe that most church conflict in Rwanda arises out of struggle for power, personality clashes and ethnic differences. Christians have a lot in common that brings them together rather than dividing them, and these are: common faith, biblical values and teachings. The Church needs to champion the cause of man being God's creature, made in his own image. It needs to realize that God made humankind and calls us to be productive. The Tutsi and the Hutu are all a part of God's creation. Because of sin, our relationship with God was marred, but God still loved the world and gave his Son to redeem it. The blood shed by Christ makes all human beings that accept and believe in him become children of God, and thus one in him. In Christ, the issues of ethnicity are demolished. Jesus is the basis of unity for all believers.

The issue of regionalism that tore Rwanda apart before the 1990 RPF attack could do it again if Rwanda's leaders are not careful. In fact, Rwanda now has more people, representing more backgrounds, than ever before. These different backgrounds could be a blessing if leaders use the giftedness of each person or community leader. That requires another demolition: that the issues of regionalism be demolished and decisions be made on the basis of merit for each person in the country.

The Church in Rwanda and Christians in general need to remember that without Christ there will be discord not only between God and humans, but also between humans. It is thus important that Rwandan Christians rededicate their lives to Christ. Not one Christian can live with another brother or sister in peace without Christ. My personal experience is that to live a victorious life free from struggles of hatred and ethnic conflicts, a person has to be broken in response to God's working and conviction in their life. As evangelist Paul Rutwe used to say, 'Christians need to be broken continually.' Breaking to build. It is a paradigm that describes the Christian life, and could take Rwanda from the edge of renewed conflict to a fresh start.

Afterword

THE MORE I think about what happened in Rwanda as put forward in this book, the more I think the situation provided a wonderful opportunity for the Rwandan people to learn from the most difficult events and situations the country has ever experienced. I also believe that there are lessons that reach beyond the Rwandan borders, especially for the Christian communities of both Africa and the West.

Christians tend to forget their true citizenship and oneness in Christ. Even those in Christian missions forget the biblical truth of humankind being created in God's image. Colonial Christian missions in Rwanda struggled to serve the Church of Jesus Christ – the colony of heaven. The Scripture states, 'Our citizenship is in heaven. And we eagerly await a Saviour from there, the Lord Jesus Christ' (Philippians 3.20). The Christian community continues to struggle in its relation to the primary mission of the Church as contrasted to allegiance to ethnic or state-expected obligations. The historical examples traced in this book demonstrate that Christians have to make their primary responsibility and priorities right before the Lord, political fallout notwithstanding.

The Catholic mission's strategy seems to have been double-minded. The desire to evangelize through traditional leadership, and failure to implement that desired strategy, led the Church into political struggles, and those struggles nurtured the whole idea of establishing the Christian kingdom they had envisioned. The Hebraic model of theocracy, which would link spiritual leaders with political power, failed to become reality in Rwanda, but made a significant impact on the political leadership. Church leaders in Africa, and elsewhere, have to be careful to avoid combining religious and political functions. Church and mission leaders must watch the relationship between church and state, as these can be dangerous for the Church. In Rwanda they have demonstrated patterns of manipulation within the Church, and the abuse of governmental relationships by the Church. Godly leaders have to recognize their dual obligations to God and to the government under which they serve. The Church lacked and continues to lack clear principles to govern its relationship with state and political leaders. A clear biblical view of the state can help the Rwandan church and its leaders formulate biblical guidelines of how to relate to the government.

The Church could seek power and support from political leaders rather than focusing on its primary mission. But that desire took the colonial Christian missionaries down the wrong path, into what continues to be a struggle in Christian ministry today: the struggle to fulfil the Great Commission, to make Christ known. Examining the colonial Christian mission, we see how the Catholic mission did not clearly distinguish between its primary mission of gospel proclamation and civic obligations. The failure to establish a favourable relationship with the Rwandan traditional leadership contributed to a change in mission strategy and led the Church to focus on politics. The result? Politics became the main agenda of church leaders, and evangelism secondary.

Church leaders are constantly tempted to fall into the role of the exploiter. In Rwanda kick-backs, the wrong use of land by mission groups, favouritism and patronage abuses by both missionaries and national church leaders are all forms of exploitation that have been practised and accepted in the Church, making it ineffective in its ministry.

The Rwandan church failed to challenge social injustices. It is sin to allow social injustice anywhere, especially in the Church; and yet there are places where Christian missions and churches have actually sought to justify the drawing of lines according to their view of the human race. The Rwandan genocide is a typical example of what can happen when we draw lines and view others as less than people made in God's image.

The Rwandan 'heroes of faith' in the genocide have reminded us of the early church Christians. Today, very few Christians are willing to suffer for Christ, and the conduct of Rwandan Christians and church leaders has important lessons for today's Christian Church. The Church has to both understand and biblically define the issues of ethnicity, race and party politics in today's pluralistic society. Where the Church does draw its lines of ethnic division, race and nationalism demands careful scrutiny. The Church failed to engage in critical and constructive collaboration with the state to bring harmony and to work against divisiveness. The Church opted instead to support both colonial and post-colonial political leaders and their evil-doing rather than steering them away from human abuses and social injustice.

As much as Christianity in Rwanda has worked energetically toward social issues that ended up becoming discriminatory in nature, I believe that Christians should use the same energy to eliminate or speak on the social issues that cause suffering. The Church cannot, however, afford to identify itself with a particular social class or political party and so compromise its prophetic message.

Early Christian missions kept Christianity as an alien religion with foreign cultural practices, and by considering Rwandan cultural practices non-Christian in nature, eradicated traditional values. The practice created a vacuum in beliefs and values of the people, especially when church leaders did not model what they taught.

Rwandan Christians have to seek the Kingdom of God first, and then build their nation on Christian principles and foundations. Only a sincere and clear commitment to God will bring Christians to live in harmony and peace with one another. Only then will the Church recover a credible prophetic voice.

1 Double Mission:
The Colonial Masters and Early Missionaries

1. Classe, L.-P. (Bishop), *Ils Trébuchaient dans les Ténèbres*. Grands Lacs, no. special, 1 March 1935.
2. Lemarchand, R., *Rwanda and Burundi*. New York, Praeger Publishers, 1970.
3. African Rights, *Rwanda: Death, Despair and Defiance*, 2nd edn. London, African Rights, 1995.

2 The Church Begins

1. Latourette, K. S., *A History of Christianity*. New York, Harper & Row, 1975, p. 1069.
2. Linden, I., *Church and Revolution in Rwanda*. New York, African Publishing Company, 1977, p. 3.
3. Kimenyi, A., *Kinyarwanda and Kirundi Names*. The Edwin Millen Press, 1989, p. 26.
4. Hiebert, P. G., *Cultural Anthropology*. Grand Rapids, Baker House, 1993, p. 54.
5. Kimenyi, *Kinyarwanda and Kirundi Names*, pp. 47–8.
6. Newbury, C., *The Cohesion of Oppression: Clientship and Ethnicity in Rwanda 1860–1960*. New York, Columbia University Press, 1988, p. 12.

3 Early Fruits of the Hard Labour

1. Lavigerie, (Cardinal), *Instruction aux missionnaires*. Namur, Grand Lacs, 1950, p. 63.
2. From 29 May 1996, interview with Kigeri V (Rwandan exiled king, now in Washington, DC).
3. Hastings, A., *African Christianity*. London, Cassell and Collier Macmillan Publishers Ltd., 1976, p. 15.
4. Mbonimana, G., *L'instauration d'un royaume Chrétien au Rwandan, 1900–1931*. Dissertation, Louvain-la Neuve, 1991.
5. Hastings, *African Christianity*, p. 6.
6. Yohannan, K. P., *Why the World Waits*. Lake Mary, Creation House, 1991, p. 23.

7. Hastings, *African Christianity*, p. 14.
8. Venn, H., 'The Organization of Native Churches' (1861), in *To Apply the Gospel: Selections from the Writings of Henry Venn*, ed. Max Warren. Grand Rapids, Eerdmans, 1971, p. 67.
9. Linden, I., *Church and Revolution in Rwanda*. New York, African Publishing Company, 1977, p. 21.
10. African Rights, *Rwanda: Death, Despair and Defiance*, 2nd edn. London, African Rights, 1995.
11. Logiest, G., *Mission au Rwanda*. Bruxelles, Didier, Hatier, 1988, p. 2.
12. ibid.
13. Church, J. E., *Quest for the Highest*. Exeter, Paternoster, 1981, p. 252.

4 The Christian Faith and European Customs

1. Hustad, D., *Jubilante*. Carol Stream, Hope Publishing Company, 1981, p. 8.
2. Allen, R. and Borror, G., *Worship: Rediscovering the Missing Jewel*. Portland, Multnomah Press, 1982, p. 163.
3. Yohannan, K. P., *Why the World Waits*. Lake Mary, Creation House, 1991, p. 24.
4. Dowden, R., Africa Editor of the *Independent*, in *Vocation for Justice*, Vol. 8 No. 2, 1994.

5 Dominance, Exploitation and the Seeds of Christianity

1. Sanders, E., 'The Hamitic Hypothesis: Its Origin and Function in Time Perspective', *Journal of African History*, 1969, pp. 521–32.

6 The Death of a Credible Christian Testimony

1. Sanders, E., 'The Hamitic Hypothesis: Its Origin and Function in Time Perspective', *Journal of African History*, 1969, pp. 521–32.
2. De Lacger, Louis, *Rwanda*, Kabgayi, 1961 edn.

8 The Corruption of Church Leadership

1. Linden, I., *Church and Revolution in Rwanda*. Manchester, Manchester University Press, 1978, p. 243.

11 Bloody Sanctuaries, Silent Leaders

1. African Rights, *Rwanda: Death, Despair and Defiance*, 2nd edn. London, African Rights, 1995.

12 Where Was God?

1. McCullum, H., *The Angels Have Left Us: The Rwanda Tragedy and the Churches*. Geneva, WCC Publications, 1995, p. 19.
2. ibid.

14 Tested and Proved

1. From a collection of interviews by Deo Gahamanyi, commissioned by the author, March 1996.

15 The Key of Confession

1. McCullum, H., *The Angels Have Left Us: The Rwanda Tragedy and the Churches*. Geneva, WCC Publications, 1995.
2. Kibaki, Mwai, quoted in David M. Gitari, *Let the Bishop Speak*. Nairobi, Uzima Publications, 1988, p. 76.
3. Gitari, David M., *Let the Bishop Speak*. Nairobi, Uzima Publications, 1988, p. 71.

16 Laying the Foundation for Reconciliation

1. Dortzbach, Karl. Quoted in *Pulse*, 23 February 1996.
2. African Rights, *Rwanda Killing the Evidence: Murder, Attacks, Arrests and Intimidation of Survivors and Witnesses*. London, African Rights, 1996.

18 Demolition

1. Coleman, R., *Dry Bones Can Live Again*. Old Tappan, Revell, 1969, p. 29.
2. Bass, Bernard M., *Leadership and Performance Beyond Expectations*. New York, The Free Press, 1985, chs. 1 and 2; quoted in Leighton Ford, *Transforming Leadership*, 1991, p. 22.

3. Ford, L., *Transforming Leadership*. Downers Grove, Intervarsity Press, 1991.
4. Fuller, H., from an address given to The Fifth Assembly of AEAM in Lusaka, Zambia, 1987.
5. See Boateng, Felix, 'African Traditions', *Journal of Black Studies*, 1978.
6. Kittel, G. and Fiendrich, G., *Theological Dictionary of the New Testament*. Grand Rapids, Eerdmans, 1967.
7. See Fafunwa, A. B., 'African Education in Perspective', in *Education in Africa: A Corporative Study*, ed. A. B. Fafunwa and J. U. Aisiku. London, George Allen and Unwin, 1982.

Index